Guitar Chord Songbook

Gospel Hymns

Guitar Chord Songbook

Contents

Amazing Grace

Words by John Newton
From a Collection of Sacred Ballads
Traditional American Melody
From Carrell and Clayton's Virginia Harmony
Arranged by Edwin O. Excell

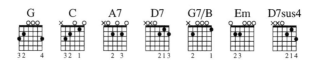

Verse 1

>   **G**   **C**   **G**
> A - mazing grace, how sweet the sound,
>
>   **A7**   **D7**
> That saved a wretch like me.
>
> **G**   **G7/B** **C**   **G**
> I once was lost but now am found,
>
>   **Em**   **D7** **G**
> Was blind but now I see.

Verse 2

>   **G**   **C**   **G**
> 'Twas grace that taught my heart to fear,
>
>   **A7**   **D7**
> And grace my fears re - lieved.
>
> **G**   **G7/B** **C**   **G**
> How precious did that grace ap - pear
>
>   **Em**   **D7**   **G**
> The hour I first be - lieved.

GUITAR CHORD SONGBOOK

Verse 3

```
        G                C      G
The Lord has prom - ised good to me,

            A7        D7sus4
His word my hope se - cures.

D7  G     G7/B     C      G
  He will my shield and portion be

   Em      G D7 G
As long as life en - dures.
```

Verse 4

```
            G            C      G
Through many dangers, toils and snares,

        A7    D7
I have al - ready come.

    G        G7/B      C       G
'Tis grace hath brought me safe thus far,

    Em        D7      G
And grace will lead me home.
```

Verse 5

```
        G               C       G
When we've been there ten thou - sand years,

        A7    D7
Bright shining as the sun,

    G      G7/B  C         G
We've no less days to sing God's praise

    Em            D7  G
Than when we'd first be - gun.
```

Are You Washed in the Blood?

Words and Music by
Elisha A. Hoffman

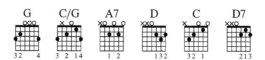

G	C/G	A7	D	C	D7
32 4	3 2 14	1 2	1 3 2	32 1	2 13

Verse 1

         G   **C/G G**
Have you been to Jesus for the cleans - ing   power?

         G   **A7**   **D**
Are you washed in the blood of the lamb?

         G   **C**
Are you fully trusting in His grace this hour?

         G   **D7** **G**
Are you washed in the blood of the Lamb?

Chorus 1

         G   **C**
Are you washed in the blood,

         G   **D G**   **D**
In the soul cleans - ing blood of the Lamb?

    D7 **G**
Are your garments spotless?

       C
Are they white as snow?

         G   **D7**   **G**
Are you washed in the blood of the Lamb?

Verse 2	G C/G G
	Are you walking daily by the Sav - ior's side?
	G A7 D
	Are you washed in the blood of the Lamb?
	G C
	Do you rest each moment in the crucified?
	G D7 G
	Are you washed in the blood of the Lamb?

Chorus 2   *Repeat Chorus 1*

Verse 3	G C/G G
	When the Bridegroom cometh will your robes be white?
	G A7 D
	Are you washed in the blood of the Lamb?
	G C
	Will your soul be ready for the mansions bright,
	G D7 G
	And be washed in the blood of the Lamb?

Chorus 3   *Repeat Chorus 1*

Verse 4	G C/G G
	Lay a - side the garments that are stained with sin,
	G A7 D
	And be washed in the blood of the Lamb.
	G C
	There's a fountain flowing for the soul unclean,
	G D7 G
	O be washed in the blood of the lamb.

Chorus 4   *Repeat Chorus 1*

At Calvary

Words by William R. Newell
Music by Daniel B. Towner

Melody:

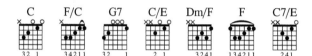

Years   I spent in van - i - ty   and pride,

C   F/C   G7   C/E   Dm/F   F   C7/E

Verse 1

C   F/C C
Years I spent in vanity and pride,

G7   C   F/C C
Caring not my Lord was cru - ci - fied,

                         F/C C   C/E Dm/F G7 C
Knowing not it was for me He   died on   Cal - va - ry.

Chorus 1

F   C
Mercy there was great and grace was free,

G7   C   C7/E
Pardon there was multi - plied to me.

F   C   C/E Dm/F G7 C
There my burdened soul found lib - erty, at   Cal - va - ry.

GUITAR CHORD SONGBOOK

Verse 2	C F/C C
	By God's Word at last my sin I learned,
	G7 C F/C C
	Then I trembled at the law I'd spurned,
	F/C C C/E Dm/F G7 C
	Till my guilty soul implor - ing turned to Cal - va - ry.

Chorus 2   *Repeat Chorus 1*

Verse 3	C F/C C
	Now I've giv'n to Jesus ev - 'ry - thing.
	G7 C F/C C
	Now I gladly own Him as my King.
	F/C C C/E Dm/F G7 C
	Now my raptured soul can on - ly sing of Cal - va - ry.

Chorus 3   *Repeat Chorus 1*

Verse 4	C F/C C
	O the love that true salva - tion's plan!
	G7 C F/C C
	O the grace that brought it down to man.
	F/C C C/E Dm/F G7 C
	O the mighty gulf that God did span at Cal - va - ry.

Chorus 4   *Repeat Chorus 1*

At the Cross

Words by Isaac Watts and Ralph E. Hudson
Music by Ralph E. Hudson

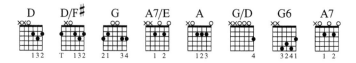

A - las! and did my Sav - ior bleed?

Verse 1

       D
A - las! and did my Savior bleed?

D/F♯ G D/F♯ A7/E D   A
And   did my   Sov - 'reign die?

D   **G/D D**
Would He devote that sa - cred head

    G6   **D**   **A7 D**
For sinners such as I?

Chorus 1

          D   **G/D D**   **A**
At the cross, at the cross where I first ___ saw the light,

     A7   **D**
And the burden of my heart rolled a - way.

     G   **D**
It was there by faith I re - ceived my sight,

    G6   **A7**   **D**
And now I am happy all the day!

Verse 2

D
Was it for crimes that I have done

D/F♯ G   D/F♯ A7/E D A
He   groaned up - on   the tree?

D   G/D D
Amazing pity, grace un - known!

     G6   D   A7 D
And love be - yond de - gree.

Chorus 2   *Repeat Chorus 1*

Verse 3

          D
Well might the sun in darkness hide

D/F♯ G   D/F♯ A7/E D   A
And   shut His   glo - ries in,

D   G/D D
When Christ, the mighty Mak - er,   died

     G6   D   A7   D
For man, the crea - ture's sin.

Chorus 3   *Repeat Chorus 1*

Verse 4

          D
But drops of grief can ne'er repay

D/F♯ G D/F♯ A7/E D A
The   debt of   love I owe.

D   G/D D
Here, Lord, I give myself a - way,

     G6   D A7 D
'Tis all that I   can do!

Chorus 4   *Repeat Chorus 1*

Blessed Assurance

Lyrics by Fanny J. Crosby
Music by Phoebe Palmer Knapp

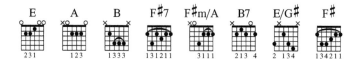

Verse 1

           E   A   E
Blessed as - surance, Jesus is mine!

                 B   F#7   B
Oh, what a fore - taste of glory di - vine!

E   A   E
Heir of salvation, purchase of God,

          A F#m/A E   B7   E
Born of His Spir - it,   washed in His blood.

Chorus 1

        E   A   E
This is my story, this is my song,

           A E/G# B   F# B
Praising my Sav - ior   all the day long.

B7   E   A   E
This is my story, this is my song,

          A F#m/A E B7   E
Praising my Sav - ior   all the day long.

Verse 2

           E   A   E
Perfect sub - mission, perfect de - light!

               B   F#7   B
Visions of rap - ture now burst on my sight.

E   A   E
Angels descending bring from a - bove

          A   F#m/A E   B7   E
Echoes of mer - cy,   whis - pers of love.

Chorus 2   *Repeat Chorus 1*

Verse 3

           E   A   E
Perfect sub - mission, all is at rest,

          B   F#7   B
I in my Sav - ior am happy and blessed.

E   A   E
Watching and waiting, looking a - bove,

         A   F#m/A E B7   E
Filled with His good - ness,   lost in His love.

Chorus 3   *Repeat Chorus 1*

Blessed Be the Name

Words by William H. Clark (verses)
and Ralph E. Hudson (refrain)
Traditional
Arranged by Ralph E. Hudson
and William J. Kirkpatrick

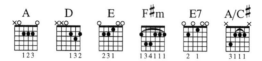

Verse 1

       A   D   A
All praise to Him who reigns a - bove,

               E
In majesty su - preme,

      A   E F#m
Who gave His Son

E   A   D
For man to die,

       A   E7 A
That He might man re - deem!

Chorus 1

A   D   A
Blessed be the name! Blessed be the name!

                  E
Blessed be the name of the Lord!

A   D   A
Blessed be the name! Blessed be the name!

         A   E7   A
Blessed be the name of the Lord!

Verse 2

      A   **D**   **A**
His name above all names shall stand,

            E
Exalted more and more.

  A   **E** **F$\sharp$m** **E**
At God the Fa - ther's

A   **D**
Own right hand,

      A   **E7** **A**
Where angel hosts a - dore.

Chorus 2   *Repeat Chorus 1*

Verse 3

      A   **D**   **A**
His name shall be the Counsel - lor,

             E
The mighty Prince of Peace.

  A E   **F$\sharp$m** **E**
Of all earth's king - doms

A   **A/C$\sharp$** **D**
Con - quer - or,

      A   **E7** **A**
Whose reign shall nev - er cease.

Chorus 3   *Repeat Chorus 1*

Brighten the Corner Where You Are

Words by Ina Duley Ogdon
Music by Charles H. Gabriel

Do not wait un - til some deed of great-ness

E   E/G#   G°7   B7/F#   B7   A

Verse 1

        E   **E/G#   G°7   B7/F#**
Do not wait until some deed of greatness you   may   do,

        B7   **E**
Do not wait to shed your light a - far.

B7   **E**   **A**
To the many duties ever near you now be true.

Chorus 1

E   **B7 E**
Brighten the corner where you are.

                B7
Brighten the corner where you are.

                E
Brighten the corner where you are.

                    A
Someone far from harbor you may guide across the bar.

E   **B7 E**
Brighten the corner where you are.

GUITAR CHORD SONGBOOK

Verse 2

   E   E/G♯ G°7 B7/F♯
Just a - bove are clouded skies that you may help to clear.

   B7   E
Let not narrow self your way de - bar,

  B7   E   A
Though in - to one heart alone may fall your song of cheer.

Chorus 2 *Repeat Chorus 1*

    E   E/G♯ G°7 B7/F♯
Verse 3
    Here for all your talent you may surely find a need.

    B7   E
Here re - flect the Bright and Morning Star.

  B7 E   A
Even from your humble hand the bread of life may feed.

Chorus 3 *Repeat Chorus 1*

Church in the Wildwood

Words and Music by
Dr. William S. Pitts

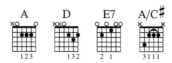

Verse 1

        A   D A   E7
There's a church in the valley by the wild - wood,

             A
No lovelier spot in the dale.

A/C# D   A
No   place is so dear to my childhood

      E7   A
As the little brown church in the vale.

Chorus 1

       A
Oh, come, come, come, come.

     D A   E7
Come to the church in the wild - wood,

             A
Oh, come to the church in the vale.

A/C# D   A
No   spot is so dear to my childhood

      E7   A
As the little brown church in the vale.

Verse 2

        A   D A   E7
Oh, come to the church in the wild - wood,

                                 A
To the trees where the wild flowers bloom,

A/C#   **D**   **A**
Where the parting hymn will be chanted,

        E7   **A**
We will weep by the side of the tomb.

Chorus 2   *Repeat Chorus 1*

Verse 3

        A   D A   E7
From the church in the valley by the wild - wood,

                       A
When day fades away into night,

A/C# **D**   **A**
I would fain from this spot of my childhood,

        E7   **A**
Wing my way to the mansions of light.

Chorus 3   *Repeat Chorus 1*

Count Your Blessings

Words by Johnson Oatman, Jr.
Music by Edwin O. Excell

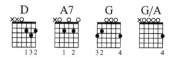

Verse 1

D   A7
When upon life's billows you are tempest tossed,

                                    D
When you are discouraged, thinking all is lost,

                                            A7
Count your many blessings, name them one by one,

                                    D   A7   D
And it will surprise you what the Lord hath done.

Chorus 1

D   A7
Count your blessings, name them one by one.

                            D
Count your blessings, see what God hath done.

        G   A7   G/A   A7
Count your blessings, name them one by one.

D   G   D   A7   D
Count your many blessings, see what God hath done.

Verse 2

D   A7
Are you ever burdened with a load of care?

                                D
Does the cross seem heavy you are called to bear?

                             A7
Count your many blessings, ev'ry doubt will fly,

                           D A7 D
And you will be singing as the days go by.

Chorus 2   *Repeat Chorus 1*

Verse 3

D   A7
When you look at others with their lands and gold,

                                D
Think that Christ has promised you His wealth untold.

                             A7
Count your many blessings, money cannot buy,

                           D   A7 D
Your reward in heaven nor your home on high.

Chorus 3   *Repeat Chorus 1*

Verse 4

D   A7
So amid the conflict, whether great or small,

                              D
Do not be discouraged, God is over all.

                           A7
Count your many blessings, angels will attend,

                           D   A7   D
Help and comfort give you to your jour - ney's end.

Chorus 4   *Repeat Chorus 1*

Does Jesus Care?

Words by Frank E. Graeff
Music by J. Lincoln Hall

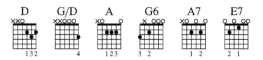

Verse 1

   D **G/D** **D** **G/D D**
Does Jesus care when my heart is pained

  A   **D**
Too deeply for mirth and song,

        G6
As the burdens press, and the cares distress,

   D   **A7** **D**
And the way grows weary and long?

Chorus 1

  A7   **D**
O yes, He cares, I know He cares.

   A **E7**   **A D A7**
His heart is touched with my grief.

    D   **G6**
When the days are weary, the long nights dreary,

  D   **A7** **D G/D D**
I know my Savior cares.

GUITAR CHORD SONGBOOK

Verse 2	D G/D D G/D D Does Jesus care when my way is dark A D With a nameless dread and fear? G6 As the daylight fades into deep nightshades, D A7 D Does He care e - nough to be near?

D   G/D   D G/D D
Does Jesus care when my way is   dark

Verse 2

    A   **D**
With a nameless dread and fear?

                 G6
As the daylight fades into deep nightshades,

       D   **A7**   **D**
Does He care e - nough to be near?

Chorus 2   *Repeat Chorus 1*

       D   **G/D**   **D** **G/D** **D**
Verse 3   Does Jesus care when I've tried and   failed

       A   **D**
To re - sist some temptation strong,

                  G6
When for my deep grief I find no relief,

       D   **A7**   **D**
Though my tears flow all the night long?

Chorus 3   *Repeat Chorus 1*

       D   **G/D**   **D** **G/D**   **D**
Verse 4   Does Jesus care when I've said good - bye

       A   **D**
To the dearest on earth to me,

                 G6
And my sad heart aches till it nearly breaks,

       D   **A7**   **D**
Is it aught to Him? Does He see?

Chorus 4   *Repeat Chorus 1*

Down At the Cross
(Glory to His Name)

Words by Elisha A. Hoffman
Music by John H. Stockton

Melody:

Down at the cross where my Sav - ior died,

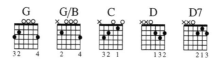

G   G/B   C   D   D7

Verse 1

```
G                    G/B     C      G
Down at the cross where my Sav - ior died,
                                    D
Down where for cleansing from sin I cried,
G               G/B   C       G
There to my heart was the blood ap - plied.
```

Chorus 1

```
G      D7  G
Glory to His  name!

C          G
Glory to His name!

           D
Glory to His name!

G               G/B   C       G
There to my heart was the blood ap - plied.

       D7  G
Glory to His name.
```

Verse 2	G G/B C G I am so won - drously saved from sin,


```
                              D
Jesus so sweetly abides with - in,

G              G/B      C        G
There at the cross where He took me in.
```

Chorus 2 *Repeat Chorus 1*

```
                   G              G/B      C            G
Verse 3            O precious foun - tain that saves from sin,

                              D
                   I am so glad that I entered in,

                   G              G/B    C        G
                   There Jesus saves me and keeps me clean.
```

Chorus 3 *Repeat Chorus 1*

```
                   G                G/B      C        G
Verse 4            Come to this foun - tain so rich and sweet,

                                   D
                   Cast thy poor soul at the Savior's feet,

                   G              G/B    C          G
                   Plunge in today and be made com - plete.
```

Chorus 4 *Repeat Chorus 1*

Down by the Riverside

African American Spiritual

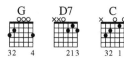

G	D7	C
32 4	213	32 1

Verse 1

     G
Gonna lay down my burden

       D7
Down by the riverside,

      G
Down by the riverside,

Down by the riverside.

Gonna lay down my burden

Down by the riverside

  D7   **G**
And study war no more.

Chorus 1

    C
I ain't gonna study war no more,

    G
I ain't gonna study war no more,

    D7   **G**
I ain't gonna study war no more.

    C
I ain't gonna study war no more,

    G
I ain't gonna study war no more,

    D7   **G**
I ain't gonna study war no more.

Verse 2
                  G
Gonna lay down my sword and shield

                  D7
Down by the riverside,

                  G
Down by the riverside,

Down by the riverside.

Gonna lay down my sword and shield

Down by the riverside

      D7   **G**
And study war no more.

Chorus 2   Repeat Chorus 1

                  G
Verse 3
Gonna try on my long white robe

                  D7
Down by the riverside,

                  G
Down by the riverside,

Down by the riverside.

Gonna try on my long white robe

Down by the riverside

      D7   **G**
And study war no more.

Chorus 3   Repeat Chorus 1

Dwelling in Beulah Land

Words and Music by
C. Austin Miles

Melody:

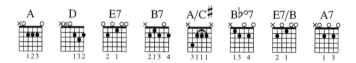

Far   a-way the   noise   of strife

A   D   E7   B7   A/C#   Bb°7   E7/B   A7

Verse 1

    A   D A   D A
Far away the noise of strife

         E7   A
Upon my ear is falling.

D   A   B7   E7
Then I know the sins of earth be - set on ev'ry hand.

A   D A   D A
Doubt and fear and things of earth

         E7   A
In vain to me are calling.

D   A/C#   D A E7 A
None of these shall move me from Beu - lah Land.

Chorus 1

        A   D A   Bb°7   E7/B
I'm living on the mountain, underneath a cloudless sky.

  E7   A   B7   E7
I'm drinking at the fountain that never shall run dry.

        A   A7   D   A
O yes, I'm feasting on the manna from a bountiful sup - ply,

        D A E7 A
For I am dwelling in Beu - lah Land.

Verse 2

A   D A   D A
Far below the storm of doubt

      E7   A
Upon the world is beating.

D   A   B7   E7
Sons of men in battle long the enemy with - stand.

A   D   A D A
Safe am I with - in the castle

      E7   A
Of God's Word re - treating,

D   A/C♯   D A E7 A
Nothing then can reach me, 'tis Beu - lah Land.

Chorus 2   *Repeat Chorus 1*

Verse 3

A   D A   D A
Let the storm - y breez - es blow,

      E7   A
Their cry can - not a - larm me.

D   A   B7   E7
I am safely sheltered here, pro - tected by God's hand.

A   D A D   A
Here the sun is al - ways shining,

      E7   A
Here there's naught can harm me.

D   A/C♯ D A   E7 A
I am safe for - ever   in Beu - lah Land.

Chorus 3   *Repeat Chorus 1*

Verse 4
```
A          D   A    D A
```
Viewing here the works of God,

```
        E7        A
```
I sink in contem - plation.

```
D           A            B7          E7
```
Hearing now His blessed voice, I see the way He planned.

```
A        D   A    D
```
Dwelling in the Spir - it,

```
A           E7      A
```
Here I learn of full sal - vation,

```
D          A/C♯ D  A    E7 A
```
Gladly will I tarry in Beu - lah Land.

Chorus 4   *Repeat Chorus 1*

Give Me That Old Time Religion

Traditional

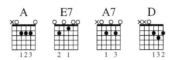

Verse 1

N.C.   **A**
Give me that old time religion,

          E7   **A**
Give me that old time re - ligion,

          A7   **D**
Give me that old time re - ligion,

    A   **E7**   **A**
It's good e - nough for me.

Verse 2

N.C. **A**
It was good for our fathers,

         E7   **A**
It was good for our fathers,

         A7   **D**
It was good for our fathers,

        A   **E7**   **A**
And it's good e - nough for me.

Verse 3

N.C. **A**
It was good for our mothers,

         E7   **A**
It was good for our mothers,

         A7   **D**
It was good for our mothers,

        A   **E7**   **A**
And it's good e - nough for me.

Verse 4   *Repeat Verse 1*

The Eastern Gate

Words and Music by
Isaiah G. Martin

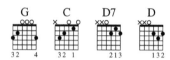

Verse 1

    G   C   G
I will meet you in the morning, just inside the Eastern Gate;

                          C   D7   G
Then be ready, faithful pilgrim, lest with you it be too late.

Chorus 1

        G
I will meet you in the morning, I will meet you in the morning,

                          D
Just inside the Eastern Gate over there.

        G
I will meet you in the morning, I will meet you in the morning,

                     D7 G
I will meet you in the morning over there.

Verse 2

```
        G                        C                    G
If you hasten off to glory, linger near the Eastern Gate;
                        C          D7              G
For I'm coming in the morning, so you'll not have long to wait.
```

Chorus 2   *Repeat Chorus 1*

Verse 3

```
        G
Keep your lamps all trimmed and burning,
        C                        G
For the Bridegroom watch and wait.
                        C      D7              G
He'll be with us at the meeting, just inside the Eastern Gate!
```

Chorus 3   *Repeat Chorus 1*

Verse 4

```
        G                        C                    G
O the joy of that glad meeting with the saints who for us wait!
                        C      D7              G
What a blessed happy meeting, just inside the Eastern Gate!
```

Chorus 4   *Repeat Chorus 1*

Footsteps of Jesus

Words by Mary B.C. Slade
Music by Asa B. Everett

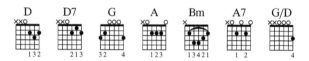

Verse 1

   D   D7 G   D
Sweetly, Lord, have we heard Thee call - ing,

           A
"Come, follow Me!"

   D   D7 G   D
And we see where Thy footprints fall - ing,

   Bm D A7 D
Lead us to Thee.

Chorus 1

   G   D   G/D D A
Footprints of Je - sus, that make the pathway glow.

   D   D7 G   D
We will fol - low the steps of Je - sus

   Bm D A7 D
Wher - e'er they go.

Verse 2

D		D7	G		D

Though the lead o'er the cold, dark moun - tains,

     A

Seeking His sheep,

D   **D7** **G**   **D**

Or along by Si - loam's foun - tains,

Bm   **D** **A7** **D**

Help - ing the weak.

Chorus 2   *Repeat Chorus 1*

Verse 3

D   **D7**   **G**   **D**

If they lead through the temple ho - ly,

     A

Preaching the Word,

D   **D7** **G**   **D**

Or in homes of the poor and low - ly,

Bm   **D** **A7** **D**

Serv - ing the Lord.

Chorus 3   *Repeat Chorus 1*

Verse 4

D   **D7**   **G**   **D**

Then at last, when on high He sees us,

     A

Our journey done,

D   **D7**   **G**   **D**

We will rest where the steps of Je - sus

Bm **D** **A7** **D**

End at His throne.

Chorus 4   *Repeat Chorus 1*

God Will Take Care of You

Words by Civilla D. Martin
Music by W. Stillman Martin

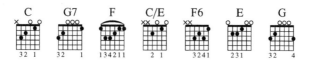

C   G7   F   C/E   F6   E   G

Verse 1

    C   G7 C
Be not dismayed whate'er be - tide,

G7   C
God will take care of you.

                           G7 C
Beneath His wings of love a - bide,

G7   C
God will take care of you.

Chorus 1

F   C
God will take care of you,

G7   C
Through ev'ry day, o'er all the way.

    C/E   F6   E
He will take care of you,

F   C   G C
God will take care of you.

Verse 2

C   G7 C
Through days of toil when heart doth fail,

G7   C
God will take care of you.

         G7 C
When dangers fierce your path as - sail,

G7   C
God will take care of you.

Chorus 2   *Repeat Chorus 1*

Verse 3

C   G7 C
All you may need He will pro - vide,

G7   C
God will take care of you.

         G7 C
Nothing you ask will be de - nied,

G7   C
God will take care of you.

Chorus 3   *Repeat Chorus 1*

Verse 4

C   G7 C
No matter what may be the test,

G7   C
God will take care of you.

         G7 C
Lean, weary one, upon His breast,

G7   C
God will take care of you.

Chorus 4   *Repeat Chorus 1*

Hallelujah, We Shall Rise

By J.E. Thomas

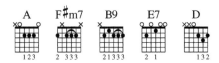

Verse 1

    A
In the resurrection morning, when the trump of God shall sound,

    F♯m7 B9   E7   A
(We shall rise.) Halle - lujah! We shall rise.

Then the saints will come rejoicing and no tears will e'er be found.

Chorus 1

    A F♯m7 B9   E7   A
We shall rise, halle - lujah! In the morning, we shall rise.

(We shall rise.) Hallelujah! (We shall rise.) Amen.

                   D   **A**
(We shall rise.) Hallelujah! In the resurrection morn - ing

When death's prison bars are broken,

    F♯m7 B9   E7   A
We shall rise, halle - lujah! We shall rise.

Verse 2   A
In the resurrection morning, what a meeting it will be.

F♯m7 B9   E7   A
(We shall rise.) Halle - lujah! We shall rise!

When our fathers and our mothers and our loved ones we shall see.

Chorus 2   *Repeat Chorus 1*

Verse 3   A
In the resurrection morning, blessed thought it is to me.

F♯m7 B9   E7   A
(We shall rise.) Halle - lujah! We shall rise.

I shall see my blessed Savior, who so freely died for me.

Chorus 3   *Repeat Chorus 1*

Verse 4   A
In the resurrection morning, we shall meet Him in the air.

F♯m7 B9   E7   A
(We shall rise.) Halle - lujah! We shall rise.

And be carried up to glory, to our home so bright and fair.

Chorus 4   *Repeat Chorus 1*

He Hideth My Soul

Words by Fanny J. Crosby
Music by William J. Kirkpatrick

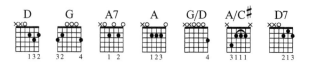

Verse 1

        D   G   D
A wonderful Savior is Jesus, my Lord,

            A7 D A
A wonderful Sav - ior to me.

A7 D   G
He hideth my soul in the cleft of the rock,

       D   A   A7 D
Where rivers of pleasure I   see.

Chorus 1

      A7   D   G/D D
He hideth my soul in the cleft of the   rock

    A7   A/C# D
That shadows a dry, thirst - y   land.

         D7 G
He hideth my life in the depths of His love

      D   A   D A7 D A7 D
And covers me there with His hand,

G D   A7   D
And covers me there with His hand.

	D G D
Verse 2	A wonderful Savior is Jesus, my Lord.

              A7 D A
He taketh my bur - den a - way.

A7 D   G
He   holdeth me up, and I shall not be moved,

     D   A   A7 D
He giveth me strength as my day.

Chorus 2   *Repeat Chorus 1*

         D   G   D

Verse 3   With numberless blessings each moment He crowns,

              A7 D A
And filled with His full - ness di - vine,

A7 D   G
I   sing in my rapture, "O glory to God,

     D   A   A7 D
For such a Re - deemer as mine!"

Chorus 3   *Repeat Chorus 1*

         D   G   D

Verse 4   When clothed in His brightness, trans - ported I rise

             A7 D A
To meet Him in clouds of the sky.

A7 D   G
His perfect salvation, His wonderful love

     D   A   A7 D
I'll shout with the millions on high.

Chorus 4   *Repeat Chorus 1*

He Keeps Me Singing

Words and Music by
Luther B. Bridgers

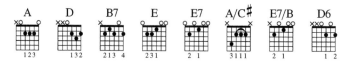

There's with - in my heart a   mel - o - dy,

A   D   B7   E   E7   A/C#   E7/B   D6

Verse 1

> A   D   A B7
> There's within my heart a   melody,
>
> E   A E7
> Jesus whispers sweet and low,
>
> A   D   A   B7
> "Fear not, I am with thee, peace be still."
>
> E   A E7 A
> In all of life's ebb and flow.

Chorus 1

> A   A/C# E7/B E
> Jesus, Je - sus,   Je - sus,
>
>   A
> Sweetest name I know.
>
>   A/C# D6   D
> Fills my ev - 'ry   long - ing,
>
> E   A E7 A
> Keeps me singing as I   go.

Verse 2

> A   D   A B7
> All my life was wrecked by sin and strife,
>
> E   A E7
> Discord filled my heart with pain.
>
> A   D   A B7
> Jesus swept a - cross the broken strings,
>
> E   A   E7 A
> Stirred the slumb'ring chords a - gain.

Chorus 2

> *Repeat Chorus 1*

Verse 3	A D A B7

<table>
<tr><td>

Verse 3

</td><td>

```
A              D     A B7
Feasting on the rich - es of His grace,

E                          A  E7
Resting 'neath His shelt'ring wing,

A            D  A  B7
Always looking on His smiling face,

E            A   E7  A
That is why I shout and sing.
```

</td></tr>
<tr><td>

Chorus 3

</td><td>

Repeat Chorus 1

</td></tr>
<tr><td>

Verse 4

</td><td>

```
A                 D     A       B7
Though sometimes He leads through waters deep,

E                 A E7
Trials fall across the way.

A                 D    A    B7
Though sometimes the path seems rough and steep,

E               A E7  A
See His footprints all the  way.
```

</td></tr>
<tr><td>

Chorus 4

</td><td>

Repeat Chorus 1

</td></tr>
<tr><td>

Verse 5

</td><td>

```
A              D    A B7
Soon He's coming back to  welcome me,

E                  A E7
Far beyond the starry sky.

A            D    A B7
I shall wing my flight to  worlds unknown,

E              A   E7 A
I shall reign with Him on  high.
```

</td></tr>
<tr><td>

Chorus 5

</td><td>

Repeat Chorus 1

</td></tr>
</table>

He's Got the Whole World in His Hands

Traditional Spiritual

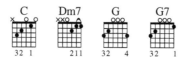

Chorus 1

        C
He's got the whole world in His hands,

        Dm7   **G** **Dm7**   **G7**
He's got the whole wide world in His hands,

        C
He's got the whole world in His hands,

        G7   **C**
He's got the whole world in His hands.

Verse 1

        C
He's got the little tiny baby in His hands,

        Dm7   **G7** **Dm7**   **G7**
He's got the little tiny baby in His hands,

        C
He's got the little tiny baby in His hands,

        G7   **C**
He's got the whole world in His hands.

Chorus 2   Repeat Chorus 1

Verse 2

           C
He's got you and me, brother, in His hands,

           Dm7   G7   Dm7   G7
He's got you and me, sister, in His hands,

           C
He's got you and me, brother, in His hands,

           G7   C
He's got the whole world in His hands.

Chorus 3   Repeat Chorus 1

Verse 3

           C
He's got ev'rybody here in His hands,

           Dm7   G7   Dm7   G7
He's got ev'rybody here in His hands,

           C
He's got ev'rybody here in His hands,

           G7   C
He's got the whole world in His hands.

Chorus 4   Repeat Chorus 1

Heavenly Sunlight

Words by Henry J. Zelley
Music by George Harrison Cook

Melody:

Walk-ing in sun - light all of my jour - ney,

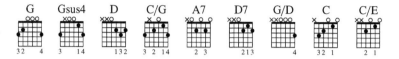

Verse 1

        G   Gsus4 G D
Walking in sunlight all of   my journey,

G C/G G   A7   D
O - ver the mountains, thru the deep vale,

        G   Gsus4 G D
Jesus has said, "I'll nev - er   for - sake thee."

G   C/G G   D7 G/D D7 G
Prom - ise divine that nev - er can fail.

Chorus 1

            C   C/E G/D C G
Heavenly sunlight, heav - en - ly sunlight,

                    A7   D
Flooding my soul with glory di - vine.

        G   Gsus4 G D
Halle - lujah! I am   re - joicing,

G   C/G G   D7 G/D D7 G
Sing - ing His praises, Je - sus is mine.

Verse 2	G Gsus4 G D

Verse 2

<pre>
          G   Gsus4 G D
Shadows a - round me, shad - ows   a - bove me,

G   C/G G   A7   D
Nev - er   conceal my Savior and Guide.

          G   Gsus4 G D
He is the light, in Him is   no darkness.

G   C/G G   D7   G/D D7 G
Ev - er   I'm walking close to   His side.
</pre>

Chorus 2   *Repeat Chorus 1*

Verse 3

<pre>
          G   Gsus4 G   D
In the bright sunlight, ev - er   re - joicing,

G   C/G G   A7   D
Press - ing   my way to mansions a - bove.

          G   Gsus4 G   D
Singing His praises, glad - ly   I'm walking,

G   C/G G   D7   G/D D7   G
Walk - ing   in sunlight, sun - light of   love.
</pre>

Chorus 3   *Repeat Chorus 1*

Higher Ground

Words by Johnson Oatman, Jr.
Music by Charles H. Gabriel

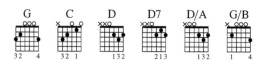

Verse 1

          G   **C**
I'm pressing on the upward way,

              G   **D**
New heights I'm gaining ev'ry day.

    G   **C**
Still praying as I'm onward bound,

             G   **D7 G**
"Lord, plant my feet on high - er   ground."

Chorus 1

             G   **D7**
Lord, lift me up and let me stand,

                G
By faith on heaven's table - land.

            D/A G/B **C**
A higher plane than I   have found,

          G   **D7 G**
Lord, plant my feet on high - er ground.

Verse 2

             G   **C**
My heart has no desire to stay

                 G   **D**
Where doubts a - rise and fears dis - may.

             G   **C**
Though some may dwell where these a - bound,

                G   **D7** **G**
My prayer, my aim, is high - er   ground.

Chorus 2   *Repeat Chorus 1*

Verse 3

             G   **C**
I want to live above the world,

                 G   **D**
Though Satan's darts at me are hurled.

             G   **C**
For faith has caught the joyful sound,

                G   **D7** **G**
The song of saints on high - er   ground.

Chorus 3   *Repeat Chorus 1*

Verse 4

             G   **C**
I want to scale the utmost height

                 G   **D**
And catch a gleam of glory bright.

             G   **C**
But still I'll pray till heav'n I've found,

                G   **D7** **G**
"Lord, lead me on to high - er   ground."

Chorus 4   *Repeat Chorus 1*

His Eye Is on the Sparrow

Words by Civilla D. Martin
Music by Charles H. Gabriel

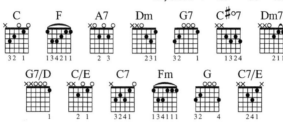

Verse 1

  C
Why should I feel discouraged?

F   **C**
Why should the shadows come?

A7   **Dm**
Why should my heart be lonely

G7   **C**
And long for heav'n and home

When Jesus is my portion?

G7 **C**   **F A7**
  My constant Friend is He.

Chorus 1

Dm **G7**   **C**
  His eye is on the sparrow,

C#°7 **Dm7**   **G7**   **C**
  And I know He watches me.

G7/D **C/E** **C7**   **F**
  His eye is on the sparrow,

Fm   **C**   **G7**   **C**
  And I know He watches me.

 G   **C**
I sing because I'm happy,

 G   **C**
I sing because I'm free.

        C7/E **F**
For His eye is on the sparrow,

Fm   **C**   **G7 C**
  And I know He watch - es me.

Verse 2

C
"Let not your heart be troubled,"

F   C
His tender words I hear.

A7   Dm
And resting on His goodness

G7   C
I lose my doubt and fear.

Though by the path He leadeth

G7   C   F A7
But one step I may see.

Chorus 2   *Repeat Chorus 1*

Verse 3

C
Whenever I am tempted,

F   C
Whenever clouds a - rise,

A7   Dm
When songs give place to sighing,

G7   C
When hope within me dies,

I draw the closer to Him,

G7   C   F A7
From care He sets me free.

Chorus 3   *Repeat Chorus 1*

I Feel Like Traveling On

Words by William Hunter
Traditional Melody
Music Arranged by James D. Vaughan

Verse 1

    G   **D7**
My heavenly home is bright and fair, I feel like traveling on.

    G   **D7**   **G**
No pain or death can enter there, I feel like traveling on.

Chorus 1

        G
Yes, I feel like traveling on.

           D7
I feel like traveling on.

   G
My heavenly home is bright and fair,

   D7   **G**
I feel like traveling on.

Verse 2

    G   **D7**
Its glitt'ring towers the sun outshine, I feel like traveling on.

    G   **D7**   **G**
That heav'nly mansion shall be mine, I feel like traveling on.

Chorus 2   *Repeat Chorus 1*

Verse 3

    G   **D7**
Let others seek a home below, I feel like traveling on.

    G   **D7**   **G**
Which flames devour or waves o'erflow, I feel like traveling on.

Chorus 3   *Repeat Chorus 1*

Verse 4

    G   **D7**
The Lord has been so good to me, I feel like traveling on.

    G   **D7**   **G**
Un - til that blessed home I see, I feel like traveling on.

Chorus 4   *Repeat Chorus 1*

Life's Railway to Heaven

Words by M.E. Abbey
Music by Charles D. Tillman

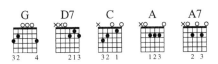

Verse 1

    G   **D7**   **G**
Life is like a mountain railroad,

      C   **G**
With an engineer that's brave.

We must make the run successful

     A   **D7**
From the cradle to the grave.

    G   **D7**   **G**
Watch the curves, the fills, the tunnels,

    C   **G**
Never falter, never quail.

Keep your hand upon the throttle,

    G   **D7**   **G**
And your eye up - on the rail.

Chorus 1

    C   **G**
Blessed Savior, Thou wilt guide us,

       A7   **D7**
Till we reach that blissful shore

    G   **C**
Where the angels wait to join us

  G   **D7** **G**
In Thy praise for - ever - more.

Verse 2

                    G   D7   G
          You will roll up grades of trial,

                    C   G
          You will cross the bridge of strife.

          See that Christ is your conductor

                    A   D7
          On this lightning train of life.

                    G   D7   G
          Always mindful of ob - struction,

                    C   G
          Do your duty, never fail.

          Keep your hand upon the throttle,

                    G   D7   G
          And your eye up - on the rail.

Chorus 2   *Repeat Chorus 1*

                    G   D7   G
Verse 3   You will often find ob - structions,

                    C   G
          Look for storms of wind and rain.

          On a fill, or curve, or trestle,

                    A   D7
          They will almost ditch your train.

                    G   D7   G
          Put your trust a - lone in Jesus,

                    C   G
          Never falter, never fail.

          Keep your hand upon the throttle,

                    G   D7   G
          And your eye up - on the rail.

Chorus 3   *Repeat Chorus 1*

Verse 4

       G   **D7**   **G**
As you roll a - cross the trestle

       C   **G**
Spanning Jordan's swelling tide,

You behold the Union Depot

    A   **D7**
Into which your train will glide.

       G   **D7**   **G**
There you'll meet the Sup'rin - tendent,

      C   **G**
God the Father, God the Son.

With the hearty, joyous plaudit,

      G   **D7**   **G**
"Weary pilgrim, welcome home."

Chorus 4   *Repeat Chorus 1*

I Have Decided to Follow Jesus

Folk Melody from India
Arranged by Auila Read

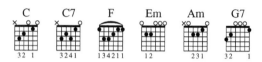

I have de - cid - ed ___ to fol-low

C   C7   F   Em   Am   G7

Verse 1

                  C
I have de - cided to follow Jesus.

C7   **F**   **C**
I have de - cided to follow Je - sus.

                    Em Am
I have decided to follow Je - sus.

           C   **G7**   **C**
No turning back, no turning back.

Verse 2

                 C
The world be - hind me, the cross before me.

C7   **F**   **C**
The world be - hind me, the cross before me.

                   Em Am
The world behind me, the cross be - fore me.

           C   **G7**   **C**
No turning back, no turning back.

Verse 3

                                     C
Though none go with me, still I will follow.

                    C7   F   C
Though none go with me, still I will fol - low.

                                               Em Am
Though none go with me, still I will fol - low.

                       C   G7   C
No turning back, no turning back.

Verse 4

                           C
Will you de - cide now to follow Jesus?

                  C7   F   C
Will you de - cide now to follow Je - sus?

                                         Em Am
Will you decide now to follow Je - sus?

                       C   G7   C
No turning back, no turning back.

I Love to Tell the Story

Words by A. Catherine Hankey
Music by William G. Fischer

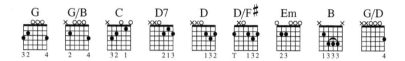

G	G/B	C	D7	D	D/F#	Em	B	G/D

Verse 1

    G   G/B C   G
I love to tell the story of   unseen things a - bove,

      D7   G   G/B D
Of Jesus and His glo - ry, of Jesus and His love.

     D/F# D7   G   Em   B
I love to tell the story be - cause I know 'tis true,

       C   G G/B D7   G/D D7   G
It satisfies my long - ings as   noth - ing   else can do.

Chorus 1

     D7   G
I love to tell the sto - ry.

    G/B C   G
'Twill be my theme in glo - ry

            G/B   C
To tell the old, old sto - ry

     G   D7   G
Of Jesus and His love.

Verse 2

```
         G                  G/B  C          G
I love to tell the story, more wonderful it seems

         D7              G                G/B  D
Than all the golden fan - cies of all our gold - en   dreams.

   D/F#  D7    G      Em                 B
I love to tell the story, it did so much for me,

         C                  G  G/B  D7  G/D  D7    G
And that is just the rea - son I     tell  it     now to thee.
```

Chorus 2   *Repeat Chorus 1*

Verse 3

```
         G                  G/B  C          G
I love to tell the story, 'tis    pleasant to re - peat

         D7                 G                G/B  D
What seems, each time I tell it, more wonderful - ly    sweet.

   D/F#  D7    G      Em                 B
I love to tell the story, for some have never heard

         C                  G  G/B  D7   G/D  D7  G
The message of salva - tion from God's own  holy Word.
```

Chorus 3   *Repeat Chorus 1*

Verse 4

```
         G                  G/B  C              G
I love to tell the story, for    those who know it best

         D7                 G                G/B  D
Seem hungering and thirst - ing to hear it like the   rest.

   D/F#  D7    G      Em                 B
And when in scenes of glory I sing the new, new song,

         C                  G  G/B  D7  G/D  D7    G
'Twill be the old, old sto - ry  that  I    have  loved so long.
```

Chorus 4   *Repeat Chorus 1*

I Must Tell Jesus

Words and Music by
Elisha A. Hoffman

Melody:

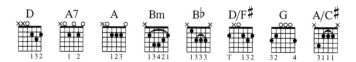

I must tell Je - sus all of my

D   A7   A   Bm   B♭   D/F#   G   A/C#

Verse 1

              D   A7 D
I must tell Jesus all of my tri - als,

                                A
I cannot bear these burdens a - lone.

D   A7 Bm
In my distress He kindly will help me,

B♭   D   A7 D
He ever loves and cares for His own.

Chorus 1

              D   D/F#   G
I must tell Jesus! I must tell Jesus!

              D   A/C#   D A
I cannot bear my burdens a - lone.

D   A7 Bm
I must tell Jesus! I must tell Je - sus!

B♭   D   A7 D
Jesus can help me, Jesus a - lone.

Verse 2

         D   **A7** **D**
I must tell Jesus all of my trou - bles,

                  A
He is a kind, compassionate Friend.

D   **A7 Bm**
If I but ask Him, He will de - liv - er,

B♭   **D**   **A7 D**
Make of my troubles quickly an end.

Chorus 2   *Repeat Chorus 1*

Verse 3

           D   **A7** **D**
O how the world to evil al - lures me.

                 A
O how my heart is tempted to sin.

D   **A7 Bm**
I must tell Jesus, and He will help me

B♭   **D**   **A7 D**
Over the world the vict'ry to win.

Chorus 3   *Repeat Chorus 1*

I Stand Amazed in the Presence

(My Savior's Love)

Words and Music by
Charles H. Gabriel

Melody:

I stand a-mazed in the pres - ence

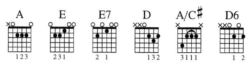

A   E   E7   D   A/C#   D6

Verse 1

        A   E
I stand amazed in the presence of Jesus,

        A   E7   A
The Naz - a - rene,

        D   A   A/C#
And wonder how He could love me,

D6   A   E7   A
A   sinner, con - demned, un - clean.

Chorus 1

A
How marvelous! How wonderful!

E
And my song shall ever be,

A
How marvelous! How wonderful

D6   A   E7   A
Is my Savior's love for me.

Verse 2

        A   E
For me it was in the garden He prayed,

        A   E7   A
"Not My will, but Thine."

        D   A   A/C#
He had no tears for His own griefs,

D6   A   E7   A
But sweatdrops of blood for mine.

Chorus 2

        Repeat Chorus 1

	A
Verse 3	In pity angels beheld Him,
	E **A** **E7 A**
	And came from the world of light
	D **A** **A/C♯**
	To comfort Him in the sor - rows
	D6 A **E7** **A**
	He bore for my soul that night.
Chorus 3	*Repeat Chorus 1*
	A
Verse 4	He took my sins and my sorrows,
	E **A** **E7 A**
	He made them His ver - y own.
	D **A** **A/C♯**
	He bore the burden to Cal - v'ry,
	D6 A **E7** **A**
	And suffered and died a - lone.
Chorus 4	*Repeat Chorus 1*
	A
Verse 5	When with the ransomed in glory
	E **A E7 A**
	His face I at last shall see,
	D **A A/C♯**
	'Twill be my joy through the ag - es
	D6 A **E7** **A**
	To sing of His love for me.
Chorus 5	*Repeat Chorus 1*

I've Got Peace Like a River

Traditional

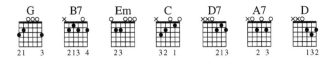

Verse 1

        G
I've got peace like a river,

B7   Em   C   D7
I've got peace like a river,

        G   Em A7   D D7
I've got peace like a river in my soul;

        G
I've got peace like a river,

B7   Em   C   D7
I've got peace like a river,

        G   Em A7 D7 G
I've got peace like a river in my soul.

Verse 2

        G
I've got love like an ocean,

B7   **Em C**   **D7**
I've got love like an ocean,

        G   **Em**   **A7**   **D** **D7**
I've got love like an ocean in my soul;

        G
I've got love like an ocean,

B7   **Em C**   **D7**
I've got love like an ocean,

        G   **Em**   **A7**   **D7** **G**
I've got love like an ocean in my soul.

Verse 3

        G
I've got joy like a fountain,

B7   **Em C**   **D7**
I've got joy like a fountain,

        G **Em** **A7**   **D** **D7**
I've got joy like a fountain in my soul;

        G
I've got joy like a fountain,

B7   **Em C**   **D7**
I've got joy like a fountain,

        G **Em** **A7**   **D7** **G**
I've got joy like a fountain in my soul.

In the Garden

Words and Music by
C. Austin Miles

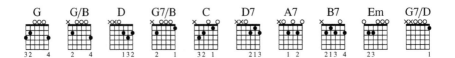

G	G/B	D	G7/B	C	D7	A7	B7	Em	G7/D

Verse 1

          G   **G/B D**
I come to the gar - den alone

         G7/B C   **G**
While the   dew is still on the roses.

         D7   **G/B D G**
And the voice I hear falling on   my ear,

        A7   **D**   **A7 D7**
The Son of God dis - clos - es.

Chorus 1

         G   **D7**
And He walks with me and He talks with me,

              G
And He tells me I am His own.

         B7   **Em G7/D C**
And the joy we share as we tar - ry   there,

        G   **D7 G**
None other has ever known.

	G G/B D

Verse 2

        G   **G/B D**
He speaks and the sound of   His voice

     G7/B C   **G**
Is so   sweet the birds stop their singing.

         D7   **G/B D G**
And the melody that He gave to me

         A7   **D**   **A7 D7**
With - in my heart is ring   -   ing.

Chorus 2   *Repeat Chorus 1*

        G   **G/B D**
Verse 3   I'd stay in the gar - den   with Him,

          G7/B C   **G**
Though the   night around me be falling.

         D7   **G/B D G**
But He bids me go, thru the voice of woe,

     A7   **D**   **A7 D7**
His voice to me is call   -   ing.

Chorus 3   *Repeat Chorus 1*

Jesus Is the Sweetest Name I Know

Words and Music by
Lela Long

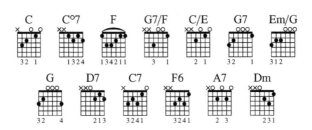

Verse 1

          C   C°7   C   F
There have been names that I have

C   G7/F C/E
Loved to   hear,

C   C°7 C   F   G7   C
But never has there been a name so   dear

G7 Em/G G7   Em/G G7
To   this   heart of   mine

C   F   C
As the name divine,

       G   D7   G7
The precious, precious name of Je - sus.

Chorus 1

C   C°7 C   F   C
Jesus is   the sweetest name I know,

        Em/G G7   F   C
And He's just   the same as His love - ly name.

        C°7 C   F   C
And that's the rea - son why I love Him so.

C7 F6   A7 Dm   G   C
O   Jesus is the sweetest name I know.

Verse 2

      C   C°7 C F
There is no name in earth or

C   G7/F C/E
Heav'n a - bove

C   C°7 C   F   G7 C
That we should give such honor and such love

G7 Em/G G7   Em/G G7
As the   bless - ed   name.

C F   C
Let us all acclaim

     G   D7   G7
That wondrous, glorious name of Je - sus.

Chorus 2   *Repeat Chorus 1*

Verse 3

      C   C°7 C   F
And someday I   shall see Him

C G7/F C/E
Face to   face

C   C°7 C F   G7   C
To thank and praise Him for His won - drous grace,

G7   Em/G G7 Em/G G7
Which He   gave to   me

C   F   C
When He made me free,

     G   D7   G7
The blessed Son of God called Je - sus.

Chorus 3   *Repeat Chorus 1*

Jesus Paid It All

Words by Elvina M. Hall
Music by John T. Grape

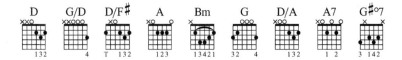

D   G/D   D/F♯   A   Bm   G   D/A   A7   G♯°7

Verse 1

      D G/D D
I hear the   Savior say,

   D/F♯ A   **Bm A D**
"Thy   strength in - deed is small.

          G/D D
Child of weak - ness, watch and pray,

D/F♯ G D/A   **A7 D**
Find   in Me thine all in   all."

Chorus 1

     G/D D
Je - sus   paid it all,

   G/D D   **A**
All to   Him I owe.

D G/D D   **D/F♯ G**
Sin had left a crim - son   stain,

G♯°7 D/A   **A7 D**
He   washed it white as snow.

GUITAR CHORD SONGBOOK

Verse 2

     D   G/D D
Lord, now in - deed I find

D/F♯ A   Bm   A D
Thy   pow'r and Thine a - lone

     G/D D
Can change the leper's spots

D/F♯ G D/A   A7 D
And _____ melt the heart of stone.

Chorus 2

Repeat Chorus 1

Verse 3

     D   G/D D
For noth - ing   good have I

D/F♯   A   Bm   A D
Where - by Thy grace to claim.

     G/D D
I'll wash my   garments white

D/F♯ G D/A   A7   D
In   the blood of Cal - v'ry's Lamb.

Chorus 3

Repeat Chorus 1

Verse 4

     D   G/D D
And when be - fore the throne

D/F♯ A   Bm A   D
I   stand In Him com - plete,

     G/D D
"Jesus died my   soul to save,"

D/F♯ G D/A   A7 D
My _____ lips shall still re - peat.

Chorus 4

Repeat Chorus 1

Just a Closer Walk with Thee

Traditional
Arranged by Kenneth Morris

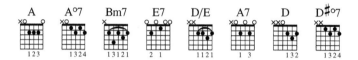

I am weak but Thou art strong.

A   A°7   Bm7   E7   D/E   A7   D   D#°7

Verse 1

    A   A°7   Bm7   E7
I am weak but Thou art   strong.

           D/E   A
Jesus, keep me from all wrong.

        A7   D   D#°7
I'll be satisfied as long

        A   E7   A
As I walk, let me walk close to Thee.

Chorus 1

    A   A°7   Bm7   E7
Just a closer walk with Thee,

           D/E   A
Grant it, Jesus, is my plea.

        A7   D   D#°7
Daily walking close to Thee,

        A   E7   A
Let it be, dear Lord, let it be.

GUITAR CHORD SONGBOOK

Verse 2

   A   A°7 Bm7 E7
Thro' this world of toil and snares,

          D/E   A
If I falter, Lord, who cares?

        A7   D   D♯°7
Who with me my burden shares?

        A   E7   A
None but Thee, dear Lord, none but Thee.

Chorus 2   *Repeat Chorus 1*

   A   A°7 Bm7 E7
Verse 3   When my feeble life is   o'er,

           D/E   A
Time for me will be no more.

        A7   D D♯°7
Guide me gently, safely o'er

        A   E7   A
To Thy kingdom shore, to Thy shore.

Chorus 3   *Repeat Chorus 1*

Just As I Am

Words by Charlotte Elliott
Music by William B. Bradbury

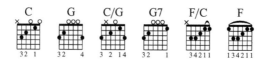

Verse 1

    C   **G**   **C**
Just as I am, with - out one plea

   G C/G G7   **F/C C**
But that Thy   blood was shed for me,

                   F
And that Thou bidd'st me come to Thee,

    C   **G**   **C**
O Lamb of God, I come, I come!

Verse 2

    C   **G**   **C**
Just as I am, and waiting not

   G C/G G7   **F/C C**
To rid my   soul of one dark blot,

                   F
To Thee whose blood can cleanse each spot,

    C   **G**   **C**
O Lamb of God, I come, I come!

Verse 3

```
        C           G          C
Just as I am, tho tossed a - bout

     G    C/G  G7      F/C  C
With many a      conflict, many a doubt.

                         F
Fighting and fears with - in, without,

     C           G        C
O Lamb of God, I come, I come!
```

Verse 4

```
        C           G           C
Just as I am, poor, wretched, blind sight,

G    C/G  G7      F/C   C
Rich - es,    healing of    the mind.

                     F
Yea, all I need in Thee to find,

     C           G        C
O Lamb of God, I come, I come!
```

Verse 5

```
        C           G        C
Just as I am, Thou wilt re - ceive,

     G    C/G  G7      F/C    C
Wilt wel - come, pardon, cleanse, relieve.

                     F
Because Thy promise I believe,

     C           G        C
O Lamb of God, I come, I come!
```

Verse 6

```
        C           G         C
Just as I am, Thy love un - known

     G    C/G  G7   F/C  C
Has bro - ken   ev'ry bar - rier down.

                     F
Now to be Thine, yes, Thine alone,

     C           G        C
O Lamb of God, I come, I come!
```

Just Over in the Gloryland

Words by James W. Acuff
Music by Emmett S. Dean

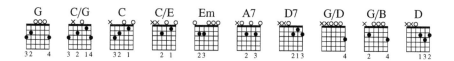

I've a home pre-pared where the saints a - bide,

G   C/G   C   C/E   Em   A7   D7   G/D   G/B   D

Verse 1

       G   C/G G   C   C/E G
I've a home pre - pared where the saints a - bide,

    Em   A7   D7
Just over in the glory - land.

       G C/G G   C   C/E G
And I long to   be by my Sav - ior's side,

    Em   G/D D7 G
Just over in the glo - ry - land.

Chorus 1

       G   D7 G
Just over in the gloryland

G/B C   C/E G
I'll   join the happy an - gel band,

    Em   A7   D   A7
Just over in the glory - land.

D   G   D7 G
  Just over in the gloryland,

G/B C   G
There with the mighty Host I'll stand,

    Em   G/D D7 G C/G G
Just over in the glo - ry - land.

Verse 2

```
        G  C/G  G          C    C/E  G
I am on  my   way to those man - sions fair,

        Em          A7    D7
Just over in the glory - land.

        G   C/G  G           C    C/E  G
There to sing God's praise and His glo - ry    share,

        Em          G/D D7 G
Just over in the glo - ry - land.
```

Chorus 2   *Repeat Chorus 1*

Verse 3

```
        G   C/G  G            C    C/E  G
What a joy - ful    thought that my Lord I'll    see,

        Em          A7    D7
Just over in the glory - land.

        G    C/G  G             C   C/E  G
And with kin - dred  saved, there for - ev - er    be,

        Em          G/D D7 G
Just over in the glo - ry - land.
```

Chorus 3   *Repeat Chorus 1*

Verse 4

```
        G     C/G   G            C   C/E  G
With the blood - washed throng I will shout and  sing,

        Em          A7    D7
Just over in the glory - land.

        G    C/G  G             C    C/E  G
Glad ho - san - nas  to Christ, the Lord and  King,

        Em          G/D D7 G
Just over in the glo - ry - land.
```

Chorus 4   *Repeat Chorus 1*

Leaning on the Everlasting Arms

Words by Elisha A. Hoffman
Music by Anthony J. Showalter

Verse 1

  A   D6
What a fellowship, what a joy divine,

  A   B9 E7
Leaning on the ever - lasting arms.

  A   D6
What a blessedness, what a peace is mine.

  A   E7 A
Leaning on the everlast - ing arms.

Chorus 1

  A   D   A   B9 E7
Leaning, leaning, safe and secure from all a - larms.

  A   D   A   E7 A
Leaning, leaning, leaning on the everlast - ing arms.

Verse 2	**A** **D6**

Verse 2

A   **D6**
O how sweet to walk in this pilgrim way,

A   **B9**   **E7**
Leaning on the ever - lasting arms.

A   **D6**
O how bright the path grows from day to day,

A   **E7** **A**
Leaning on the everlast - ing arms.

Chorus 2   *Repeat Chorus 1*

Verse 3

A   **D6**
What have I to dread, what have I to fear,

A   **B9**   **E7**
Leaning on the ever - lasting arms?

A   **D6**
I have blessed peace with my Lord so near,

A   **E7** **A**
Leaning on the everlast - ing arms.

Chorus 3   *Repeat Chorus 1*

The Lily of the Valley

Words by Charles W. Fry
Music by William S. Hays

I have found a friend in Je- sus, He's

E   A   E/G♯   B   F♯m/A   B7   E7/G♯

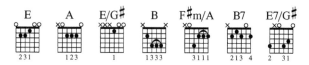

Verse 1

      E   A E   A   E
I have found a friend in Jesus, He's ev'rything to me.

            A   E/G♯ E B
He's the fairest of ten thou - sand to my soul.

    E A E   A   E
The Lily of the Valley, in Him alone I see,

          F♯m/A   E B7 E
All I need to cleanse and make me ful - ly   whole.

E7/G♯ A   E
In   sorrow He's my comfort, in trou - ble He's my stay.

        A E/G♯ E B
He tells me ev'ry care on Him to roll.

Chorus 1

      E A E
He's the Lily of the Valley,

  A   E
The Bright and Morning Star.

       F♯m/A E B7 E
He's the fairest of ten thousand to my soul.

Verse 2

```
         E    A   E        A           E
He all my griefs has taken and all my sorrows borne.

                     A   E/G♯      E  B
In temptation He's my strong and might - y  tow'r.

         E    A   E        A           E
I have all for Him forsaken, and all my idols torn from my heart,

         F♯m/A   E  B7  E
And now He keeps me by his pow'r.

E7/G♯ A                              E
Though all the world forsake me and Sa - tan tempt me sore,

                 A    E/G♯     E  B
Through Jesus I shall safe - ly reach the goal.
```

Chorus 2   *Repeat Chorus 1*

Verse 3

```
         E    A   E        A           E
He will never, nev - er leave me nor yet forsake me here,

                 A E/G♯      E  B
While I live by faith and do His bless - ed will.

    E    A   E          A             E
A wall of fire about me, I've nothing now to fear,

                 F♯m/A  E   B7    E
With His manna He my hungry  soul shall fill.

E7/G♯ A                          E
Then     sweeping up to glory I'll see His blessed face

                 A   E/G♯      E  B
Where rivers of de - light shall ev - er roll.
```

Chorus 3   *Repeat Chorus 1*

Little Is Much When God Is in It

Words by Mrs. F.W. Suffield
and Dwight Brock
Music by Mrs. F.W. Suffield

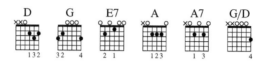

Verse 1

      D
In the harvest field now ripened,

G   **D**   **E7**   **A**
There is work for all to do.

A7   **D**
Hark, the voice of God is calling,

G   **D**   **A7 D**
To the harvest call - ing you.

Chorus 1

D   **G/D D**
Little is much when God is in it.

      G/D D   **A**
Labor not for   wealth or fame.

A7   **D**
There's a crown, and you can win it

G   **D**   **A7 D**
If you go in Je - sus' name.

Verse 2	**D** Does the place you're called to labor
	G D E7 A Seem so small and little - known?
	A7 D It is great if God is in it,
	G D A7 D And He'll not forget His own.
Chorus 2	*Repeat Chorus 1*
Verse 3	**D** Are you laid aside from service,
	G D E7 A Body worn from toil and care?
	A7 D You can still be in the battle
	G D A7 D In the sacred place of prayer.
Chorus 3	*Repeat Chorus 1*
Verse 4	**D** When the conflict here is ended
	G D E7 A And our race on earth is run
	A7 D He will say, if we are faithful,
	G D A7 D "Welcome home, my child, well done."
Chorus 4	*Repeat Chorus 1*

Love Lifted Me

Words by James Rowe
Music by Howard E. Smith

Melody:

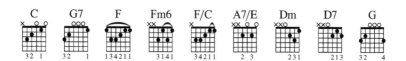

C   G7   F   Fm6   F/C   A7/E   Dm   D7   G

Verse 1

```
    C                                    G7
I was sinking deep in sin, far from the peaceful shore.
                                      C
Very deeply stained within, sinking to rise no more.
                                             F
But the Master of the sea heard my despairing cry,
             Fm6  C       F   C  G7  C
From the wa - ters   lifted me, now safe am I.
```

Chorus 1

```
         G7   C F/C  C           F  A7/E Dm
Love lifted me! _____ Love lifted me!

F           C             D7       G  G7
When nothing else could help, love lifted me.

C   G7   C F/C  C           F  A7/E Dm
Love lifted me! _____ Love lifted me!

F           C                       G7  C
When nothing else could help me, love lift - ed  me.
```

| | C   G7 |
| *Verse 2* | All my heart to Him I give, ever to Him I'll cling. |

| | C |
| | In His blessed presence live, ever His praises sing. |

| | F |
| | Love so mighty and so true merits my soul's best songs. |

| | **Fm6 C**   **F C   G7   C** |
| | Faithful lov - ing   service, too, to Him be - longs. |

Chorus 2   *Repeat Chorus 1*

| | C   G7 |
| *Verse 3* | Souls in danger, look above, Jesus completely saves. |

| | C |
| | He will lift you by His love out of the angry waves. |

| | F |
| | He's the Master of the sea, billows His will o - bey. |

| | **Fm6 C**   **F C   G7 C** |
| | He your Sav - ior   wants to be; be saved to - day. |

Chorus 3   *Repeat Chorus 1*

The Love of God

Words and Music by
Frederick M. Lehman

Melody:

The love of God is great-er

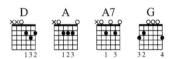

D   A   A7   G

Verse 1

        D   **A**   **D**
The love of God is greater far than tongue or pen can ever tell.

                         A7   **D**
It goes beyond the highest star and reaches to the lowest hell.

      G   **D**   **A A7 D**
The guilty pair, bowed down with care, God gave His Son to   win.

      G   **D**   **A7**   **D**
His erring child He recon - ciled and pardoned from his sin.

Chorus 1

D **G**   **D**
O love of God, how rich and pure,

          A   **D**
How measure - less and strong.

       G   **D**
It shall for - evermore en - dure,

       A7   **D**
The saints' and angels' song.

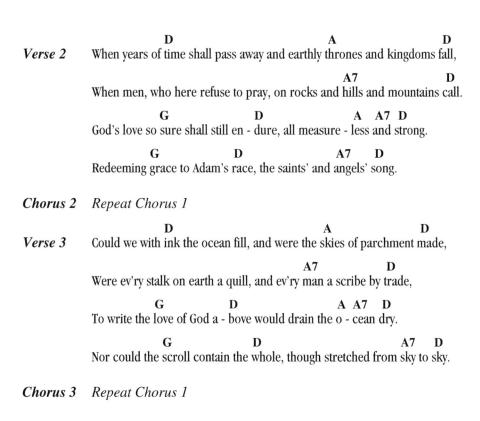

Verse 2

                    D   A   D

When years of time shall pass away and earthly thrones and kingdoms fall,

                                 A7   D

When men, who here refuse to pray, on rocks and hills and mountains call.

           G   D   A A7 D

God's love so sure shall still en - dure, all measure - less and strong.

           G   D   A7   D

Redeeming grace to Adam's race, the saints' and angels' song.

Chorus 2   *Repeat Chorus 1*

Verse 3

           D   A   D

Could we with ink the ocean fill, and were the skies of parchment made,

                        A7   D

Were ev'ry stalk on earth a quill, and ev'ry man a scribe by trade,

           G   D   A A7 D

To write the love of God a - bove would drain the o - cean dry.

           G   D   A7   D

Nor could the scroll contain the whole, though stretched from sky to sky.

Chorus 3   *Repeat Chorus 1*

My Savior First of All

Words by Fanny J. Crosby
Music by John R. Sweney

Melody:

When my life-work is end-ed and I

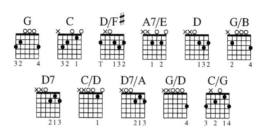

Verse 1

        G   **C**   **G**
When my lifework is ended and I cross the swelling tide,

                       D/F♯ A7/E D
When the bright and glorious morning I   shall   see,

G   **G/B C**
I shall know my Redeemer when I reach the other side,

       G   **D7**   **C/D D7**   **G**
And His smile will be the first to wel - come me.

Chorus 1

        D7   **C/D D7 G**
I shall know Him, I   shall know Him,

                 D7/A G D/F♯ A7/E D
And redeemed by His side _____ I   shall stand.

G/D D7 G   **C/G G   C**
I   shall know Him, I   shall know Him

       G   **D** **C/D D7 G**
By the prints of the nails in   His hand.

Verse 2

          G   C   G
O the soul thrilling rapture when I view His blessed face,

                    D/F♯ A7/E D
And the luster of His kindly beam - ing   eye.

G   G/B   C
How my full heart will praise Him for the mercy, love and grace

             G   D7   C/D D7 G
That pre - pare for me a mansion in   the sky.

Chorus 2   *Repeat Chorus 1*

Verse 3

          G   C   G
O the dear ones in glory, how they beckon me to come,

                    D/F♯ A7/E D
And our parting at the river I   re - call.

G   G/B   C
To the sweet vales of Eden they will sing my welcome home,

             G   D7   C/D D7 G
But I long to meet my Savior first of all.

Chorus 3   *Repeat Chorus 1*

Verse 4

          G   C   G
Thro' the gates to the city in a robe of spotless white,

                    D/F♯ A7/E D
He will lead me where no tears will ev - er   fall.

G   G/B   C
In the glad song of ages I shall mingle with delight,

             G   D7   C/D D7 G
But I long to meet my Savior first of all.

Chorus 4   *Repeat Chorus 1*

Near the Cross

Words by Fanny Crosby
Music by William H. Doane

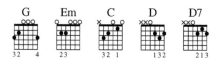

Je - sus, keep me near the cross,

Verse 1

G   Em   C
Jesus, keep me near the cross,

G   D
There a precious fountain,

G   Em   C
Free to all, a healing stream,

G   D7   G
Flows from Calv'ry's moun - tain.

Chorus 1

G   C
In the cross, in the cross

G   C   D
Be my glory ever,

G   Em   C
Till my raptured soul shall find

G   D7 G
Rest beyond the riv - er.

GUITAR CHORD SONGBOOK

	G Em C
Verse 2	Near the cross, a trembling soul,

G   D
Love and mercy found me.

G   Em   C
There the bright and morning star

G   D7   G
Sheds its beams a - round me.

Chorus 2   *Repeat Chorus 1*

G   Em   C
Verse 3   Near the cross! Oh, Lamb of God,

G   D
Bring its scenes be - fore me.

G   Em   C
Help my walk from day to day,

G   D7 G
With its shadows o'er me.

Chorus 3   *Repeat Chorus 1*

G   Em   C
Verse 4   Near the cross I'll watch and wait,

G   D
Hoping, trusting ever,

G   Em   C
Till I reach the golden strand

G   D7 G
Just beyond the riv - er.

Chorus 4   *Repeat Chorus 1*

A New Name in Glory

Words and Music by
C. Austin Miles

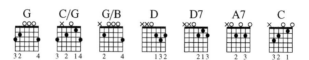

I was once a sin-ner, but I came,

Verse 1

      G   C/G G   G/B D G
I was once a sin - ner, but I came,

D7   **G**
Pardon to receive from my Lord.

                 C/G G G/B D G
This was freely giv - en, and I found

A7   **D7**
That He always kept His word.

Chorus 1

                G
There's a new name written down in glory,

          C   **G**
And it's mine, O yes, it's mine.

          D7   **G**
And the white robed angels sing the story,

     A7   **D7**
"A sinner has come home."

                G
For there's a new name written down in glory,

          C   **G**
And it's mine, O yes, it's mine.

          C   **G**   **C**
With my sins forgiven I am bound for heav - en,

G   **D7**   **G**
Never - more to roam.

Verse 2

```
G            C/G   G  G/B  D  G
I was humbly kneel - ing at    the cross,

D7                          G
Fearing naught but God's angry frown,

          C/G  G      G/B  D  G
When the heavens o  -  pened and I   saw

A7                     D7
That my name was written down.
```

Chorus 2   *Repeat Chorus 1*

Verse 3
```
G             C/G  G    G/B   D  G
In the Book 'tis writ - ten, "Saved by grace."

D7                      G
O the joy that came to my soul.

        C/G  G  G/B  D  G
Now I am for - giv - en, and  I   know

A7                    D7
By the blood I am made whole.
```

Chorus 3   *Repeat Chorus 1*

No, Not One!

Words by Johnson Oatman, Jr.
Music by George C. Hugg

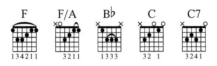

Verse 1

    F   **F/A** **B♭**   **F**
There's not a friend like the lowly Je - sus,

                C   **F** **C7** **F**
No, not one! No, not one!

                            F/A **B♭**   **F**
None else could heal all our soul's diseas - es,

                C   **F** **C7** **F**
No, not one! No, not one!

Chorus 1

    F   **C7**   **F**
Jesus knows all about our strug - gles,

                          C
He will guide till the day is done.

    F   **F/A** **B♭**   **F**
There's not a friend like the lowly Je - sus,

                C   **F** **C7** **F**
No, not one! No, not one!

Verse 2

    F   **F/A** **B♭**   **F**
No friend like Him is so high and ho - ly,

                C   **F** **C7** **F**
No, not one! No, not one!

                      F/A **B♭**   **F**
And yet no friend is so meek and low - ly,

                C   **F** **C7** **F**
No, not one! No, not one!

Chorus 2   *Repeat Chorus 1*

Verse 3

    F   F/A   B♭   F
There's not an hour that He is not near us,

        C   F C7 F
No, not one! No, not one!

                F/A   B♭   F
No night so dark but His love can cheer us,

        C   F C7 F
No, not one! No, not one!

Chorus 3   *Repeat Chorus 1*

    F   F/A   B♭   F
Verse 4   Did ever saint find this friend forsake him?

        C   F C7 F
No, not one! No, not one!

             F/A   B♭   F
Or sinner find that He would not take him?

        C   F C7 F
No, not one! No, not one!

Chorus 4   *Repeat Chorus 1*

    F   F/A   B♭   F
Verse 5   Was e'er a gift like the Savior giv - en?

        C   F C7 F
No, not one! No, not one!

            F/A B♭   F
Will He refuse us a home in heav - en?

        C   F C7 F
No, not one! No, not one!

Chorus 5   *Repeat Chorus 1*

Nothing But the Blood

Words and Music by
Robert Lowry

What can wash a - way my sin?

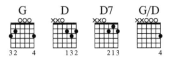

Verse 1

    G   **D G**
What can wash a - way my sin?

            D7 G
Nothing but the blood of Je - sus.

        D G
What can make me whole again?

            D7 G
Nothing but the blood of Je - sus.

Chorus 1

G   **D**   **G**
Oh, pre - cious is the flow

D7   **G/D D**   **G**
That makes me   white as snow.

     D G
No oth - er fount I know,

           D7 G
Nothing but the blood of Je - sus.

Verse 2

G   D   G
For my par - don this I see,

                     D7 G
Nothing but the blood of Je - sus.

                D   G
For my cleans - ing, this my plea,

                     D7 G
Nothing but the blood of Je - sus.

Chorus 2

Repeat Chorus 1

Verse 3

G   D G
Nothing can for sin atone,

                     D7 G
Nothing but the blood of Je - sus.

                D G
Naught of good that I have done,

                     D7 G
Nothing but the blood of Je - sus.

Chorus 3

Repeat Chorus 1

Verse 4

G   D G
This is all my hope and peace,

                     D7 G
Nothing but the blood of Je - sus.

                D G
This is all my righteousness,

                     D7 G
Nothing but the blood of Je - sus.

Chorus 4

Repeat Chorus 1

Oh, How I Love Jesus

Words by Frederick Whitfield
Traditional American Melody

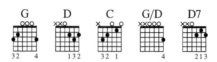

Verse 1

      G   D   G
There is a name I love to hear, I love to sing its worth.

                          C   G/D D7 G
It sounds like music in my ear, the sweetest name on earth.

Chorus 1

  G   D7   G
Oh, how I love Jesus! Oh, how I love Jesus!

                    C   G/D D7   G
Oh, how I love Jesus, be - cause he first loved me.

Verse 2

  G   D   G
It tells me of a Savior's love, who died to set me free.

                      C   G/D D7 G
It tells me of His precious blood, the sinner's per - fect plea.

Chorus 2   *Repeat Chorus 1*

Verse 3

  G   D   G
It tells me what my Father hath in store for ev'ry day.

                        C   G/D D7 G
And though I tread a darksome path, yields sunshine all   the way.

Chorus 3   *Repeat Chorus 1*

Verse 4

  G   D   G
It tells of One whose loving heart can feel my deepest woe,

                      C   G/D D7 G
Who in each sorrow bears a part that none can bear be - low.

Chorus 4   *Repeat Chorus 1*

Revive Us Again

Words by William P. MacKay
Music by John J. Husband

Melody:

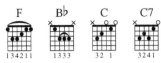

We praise Thee, O God, for the

F   Bb   C   C7

134211   1333   32 1   3241

Verse 1

    F
We praise Thee, O God, for the Son of Thy love,
       Bb   F   C
For Jesus, who died and is now gone above.

Chorus 1

F   Bb F
Halle - lu - jah! Thine the glory!
   Bb   F   C
Halle - lu - jah! A - men!
F   Bb F
Halle - lu - jah! Thine the glory!
  Bb   F C7 F
Re - vive us a - gain.

Verse 2

    F
We praise Thee, O God, for Thy Spirit of Light,
       Bb   F   C
Who has shown us our Sav - ior and scat - tered our night.

Chorus 2   *Repeat Chorus 1*

Verse 3

    F
All glory and praise to the Lamb that was slain,
       Bb   F   C
Who has borne all our sins and has cleansed ev'ry stain.

Chorus 3   *Repeat Chorus 1*

Verse 4

    F
Re - vive us again, fill each heart with Thy love.
       Bb   F   C
May each soul be re - kin - dled with fire from above.

Chorus 4   *Repeat Chorus 1*

The Old Rugged Cross

Words and Music by
Rev. George Bennard

Melody:

On a hill far a - way stood an

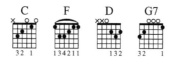

Verse 1

      C   F
On a hill far away stood an old rugged cross,

D G7   C
The emblem of suff'ring and shame.

                               F
And I love that old cross, where the dearest and best

D G7   C
For a world of lost sinners was slain.

Chorus 1

      G7   C
So I'll cherish the old rugged cross

        F   C
Till my trophies at last I lay down.

                        F
I will cling to the old rugged cross,

          C   G7   C
And ex - change it some - day for a crown.

Verse 2
         C   **F**
O that old rugged cross, so de - spised by the world,

D   **G7**   **C**
Has a wondrous attraction for me.

                       F
For the dear Lamb of God left His glory above

D G7   **C**
To bear it to dark Calva - ry.

Chorus 2   *Repeat Chorus 1*

Verse 3
         C   **F**
In the old rugged cross, stained with blood so divine,

D G7   **C**
A wondrous beauty I see.

                      F
For 'twas on that old cross Jesus suffered and died

D G7   **C**
To pardon and sanctify me.

Chorus 3   *Repeat Chorus 1*

Verse 4
         C   **F**
To the old rugged cross I will ever be true,

D G7   **C**
Its shame and reproach gladly bear.

                      F
Then He'll call me someday to my home far away,

D   **G7**   **C**
Where His glory forever I'll share.

Chorus 4   *Repeat Chorus 1*

On Jordan's Stormy Banks

Words by Samuel Stennett
Traditional American Melody
Arranged by Rigdon M. McIntosh

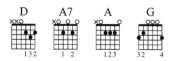

Verse 1

    D   **A7**
On Jordan's stormy banks I stand

    D   **A**
And cast a wishful eye

A7 D
To   Canaan's fair and happy land,

      G   **D**   **A7**   **D**
Where ___ my pos - sessions lie.

Chorus 1

     D   **A7**
I am bound for the Promised Land,

     D   **A**
I am bound for the Promised Land.

A7 D
O   who will come and go with me?

 G **D**   **A7**   **D**
I am bound for the Promised Land.

Verse 2

    D   A7
All o'er those wide ex - tended plaines

        D   A
Shines one eternal day.

A7   D
There God the Son forever reigns

       G D   A7   D
And ___ scatters night a - way.

Chorus 2   *Repeat Chorus 1*

Verse 3

    D   A7
No chilling winds nor pois'nous breath

        D   A
Can reach that healthful shore.

A7   D
Sick - ness and sorrow, pain and death

       G D   A7   D
Are ___ felt and feared no more.

Chorus 3   *Repeat Chorus 1*

Verse 4

    D   A7
When shall I reach that happy place

        D   A
And be forever blest?

A7   D
When shall I see my Father's face

       G D   A7   D
And ___ in His bosom rest?

Chorus 4   *Repeat Chorus 1*

Pass Me Not, O Gentle Savior

Words by Fanny J. Crosby
Music by William H. Doane

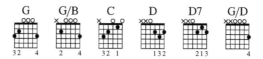

Verse 1

G   G/B   C   G   G/B
Pass me   not, O gentle Sav - ior,

D   G/B   D   G
Hear my hum - ble cry.

      G/B   C   G   G/B
While on   others Thou art call - ing,

D7   G/D   D7   G
Do not pass me by.

Chorus 1

G   C   G   G/B   D
Savior, Savior, hear my hum - ble   cry.

G   G/B   C   G   G/B
While on   others Thou art call - ing,

D7   G/D   D7   G
Do not pass me by.

Verse 2

```
G  G/B C            G    G/B
```
Let me   at the throne of mer - cy

```
D    G/B  D   G
```
Find a sweet re - lief.

```
    G/B C              G   G/B
```
Kneel - ing there in deep con - tri - tion,

```
D7      G/D  D7  G
```
Help my un - be - lief.

Chorus 2   *Repeat Chorus 1*

Verse 3
```
G     G/B C        G    G/B
```
Trust - ing   only in Thy mer - it,

```
D      G/B  D   G
```
Would I seek Thy face.

```
   G/B  C                G   G/B
```
Heal my   wounded, broken spir - it,

```
D7      G/D  D7  G
```
Save me by   Thy grace.

Chorus 3   *Repeat Chorus 1*

Verse 4
```
G    G/B C            G    G/B
```
Thou, the   Spring of all my com - fort,

```
D        G/B  D  G
```
More than life   to me,

```
    G/B  C              G   G/B
```
Whom have I on earth be - side Thee?

```
D7      G/D   D7  G
```
Whom in heav'n but Thee?

Chorus 4   *Repeat Chorus 1*

Precious Memories

Words and Music by
J.B.F. Wright

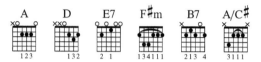

Verse 1

    A   **D**   **A**
Precious mem'ries, unseen an - gels,

    E7 **F♯m**   **B7**   **E7**
Sent from somewhere to my soul.

    A   **D**   **A**
How they linger, ever near me,

    A/C♯ **E7** **F♯m A** **E7** **A**
And the   sa - cred past un - fold.

Chorus 1

    A
Precious mem'ries, how they linger,

D   **A**
How they ever flood my soul.

         D   **A**
In the stillness of the mid - night,

    A/C♯ **E7** **F♯m A**   **E7** **A**
Pre - cious sa - cred scenes un - fold.

Verse 2

    A   D   A
Precious father, loving moth - er,

    E7 F♯m   B7   E7
Fly a - cross the lonely years,

    A   D   A
To old home scenes of my child - hood,

    A/C♯ E7   F♯m A E7 A
With fond   mem - o - ries ap - pear.

Chorus 2   *Repeat Chorus 1*

Verse 3

    A   D   A
As I travel on life's path - way,

    E7 F♯m   B7   E7
Know not what the years may hold.

    A   D   A
As I ponder, hope grows fon - der,

    A/C♯ E7   F♯m A   E7 A
Pre - cious mem - 'ries flood my soul.

Chorus 3   *Repeat Chorus 1*

Rock of Ages

Words by Augustus M. Toplady
V.1,2,4 altered by Thomas Cotterill
Music by Thomas Hastings

Melody:

Rock of Ag - es, cleft for me,

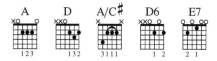

Verse 1

     A   **D**   **A**
Rock of Ages, cleft for me,

A/C# **D6** **A**   **E7** **A**
Let   me hide myself in Thee.

      E7   **A**
Let the water and the blood

        E7   **A**
From Thy wounded side which flowed

    D **A**   **D**   **A**
Be of sin the double cure,

A/C# **D6** **A**   **E7** **A**
Save   from wrath and make me pure.

Verse 2

       A   **D** **A**
Could my tears for - ever flow,

A/C# **D6** **A**   **E7**   **A**
Could   my zeal no lan - guor know,

        E7   **A**
These for sin could not a - tone,

         E7   **A**
Thou must save, and Thou a - lone.

    D **A**   **D**   **A**
In my hand no price I bring,

A/C# **D6** **A**   **E7** **A**
Sim - ply to Thy cross I   cling.

Verse 3

     A   **D**   **A**
Nothing in my hand I bring,

A/C♯ **D6** **A**   **E7** **A**
Sim - ply to Thy cross I   cling.

      E7   **A**
Naked, come to Thee for dress,

      E7   **A**
Helpless, look to Thee for grace.

    D A   **D**   **A**
Foul, I to the fountain fly,

A/C♯ **D6** **A**   **E7 A**
Wash me, Savior, or I die.

Verse 4

     A   **D**   **A**
While I draw this fleeting breath,

A/C♯ **D6** **A**   **E7 A**
When my eyes shall close in death,

     E7   **A**
When I rise to worlds un - known

     E7   **A**
And be - hold Thee on Thy throne,

    D A   **D**   **A**
Rock of Ages, cleft for me,

A/C♯ **D6** **A**   **E7 A**
Let   me hide myself in Thee.

Send the Light

Words and Music by
Charles H. Gabriel

There's a call comes ring-ing o'er the rest-less wave,

G   D7

Verse 1

      G
There's a call comes ringing o'er the restless wave,

    D7   **G**
"Send the light! Send the light!"

There are souls to rescue, there are souls to save.

    D7   **G**
Send the light! Send the light!

Chorus 1

      G
Send the light, the blessed gospel light.

   D7   **G**
Let it shine from shore to shore.

Send the light, the blessed gospel light,

   D7   **G**
Let it shine forever - more.

Verse 2	**G**
	We have heard the Macedonian call today,
	D7 **G**
	"Send the light! Send the light!"
	And a golden off'ring at the cross we lay.
	D7 **G**
	Send the light! Send the light!

Verse 2

         G
We have heard the Macedonian call today,

         D7   **G**
"Send the light! Send the light!"

And a golden off'ring at the cross we lay.

         D7   **G**
Send the light! Send the light!

Chorus 2

Repeat Chorus 1

Verse 3

         G
Let us pray that grace may ev'rywhere abound,

         D7   **G**
"Send the light! Send the light!"

And a Christ-like Spirit ev'rywhere be found.

         D7   **G**
Send the light! Send the light!

Chorus 3

Repeat Chorus 1

Verse 4

         G
Let us not grow weary in the work of love,

         D7   **G**
"Send the light! Send the light!"

Let us gather jewels for a crown above.

         D7   **G**
Send the light! Send the light!

Chorus 4

Repeat Chorus 1

Shall We Gather at the River?

Words and Music by
Robert Lowry

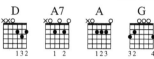

Shall we gath - er at the riv - er,

D	A7	A	G

Verse 1

D   A7
Shall we gather at the river, where bright angel feet have trod,

D   A   A7   D
With its crystal tide forever flowing by the throne of God?

Chorus 1

G   D
Yes, we'll gather at the river,

A7   D
The beautiful, the beautiful river.

G   D
Gather with the saints at the river

A   A7   D
That flows by the throne of God.

Verse 2

D   A7
On the bosom of the river, where the Savior King we own,

D   A   A7   D
We shall meet, and sorrow never 'neath the glory of the throne.

Chorus 2   *Repeat Chorus 1*

Verse 3

D   A7
Ere we reach the shining river, lay we ev'ry burden down.

D   A   A7   D
Grace our spirits will deliver and pro - vide a robe and crown.

Chorus 3   *Repeat Chorus 1*

Verse 4

D   A7
Soon we'll reach the shining river, soon our pilgrimage will cease.

D   A   A7 D
Soon our happy hearts will quiver with the melo - dy of peace.

Chorus 4   *Repeat Chorus 1*

There Is a Balm in Gilead

African-American Spiritual

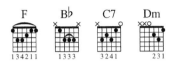

There _ is a balm in Gil - e - ad

F B♭ C7 Dm

Chorus 1

F   B♭   F C7
There is a balm in Gilead to make the wound - ed whole.

F   C7   F
There is a balm in Gilead to heal the sin - sick soul.

Verse 1

F   B♭   F   C7
Sometimes I feel dis - couraged, and think my works in vain,

    F   B♭   F   C7   Dm B♭
But then the Holy Spirit re - vives my soul a - gain.

Chorus 2   *Repeat Chorus 1*

Verse 2

F   B♭   F   C7
Don't ever feel dis - couraged, for Jesus is your friend.

    F   B♭   F   C7   Dm B♭
And if you lack for knowledge, He'll not re - fuse to lend.

Chorus 3   *Repeat Chorus 1*

Verse 3

F   B♭   F   C7
If you cannot preach like Peter, if you cannot pray like Paul,

    F   B♭   F   C7   Dm B♭
You can tell the love of Jesus and say, "He died for all."

Chorus 4   *Repeat Chorus 1*

Since Jesus Came Into My Heart

Words by Rufus H. McDaniel
Music by Charles H. Gabriel

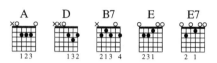

What a won-der-ful change in my life

Verse 1

         A
What a wonderful change in my life has been wrought

     D   **A**
Since Jesus came into my heart.

I have light in my soul for which long I had sought,

     B7   **E A E7**
Since Jesus came into my heart.

Chorus 1

         A
Since Jesus came into my heart,

     D   **A**
Since Jesus came into my heart,

Floods of joy o'er my soul like the sea billows roll,

D   **A**   **E7 A**
Since Jesus came into my heart.

Verse 2

         A
I have ceased from my wand'ring and going astray

     D   **A**
Since Jesus came into my heart.

And my sins, which were many, are all washed away,

     B7   **E A E7**
Since Jesus came into my heart.

Chorus 2   *Repeat Chorus 1*

Verse 3	**A** I'm pos - sessed of a hope that is steadfast and sure, **D** **A** Since Jesus came into my heart. And no dark clouds of doubt now my pathway obscure, **B7** **E A E7** Since Jesus came into my heart.
Chorus 3	*Repeat Chorus 1*
Verse 4	**A** There's a light in the valley of death now for me, **D** **A** Since Jesus came into my heart. And the gates of the City beyond I can see, **B7** **E A E7** Since Jesus came into my heart.
Chorus 4	*Repeat Chorus 1*
Verse 5	**A** I shall go there to dwell in that City, I know, **D** **A** Since Jesus came into my heart. And I'm happy, so happy, as onward I go, **B7** **E A E7** Since Jesus came into my heart.
Chorus 5	*Repeat Chorus 1*

Standing on the Promises

Words and Music by
R. Kelso Carter

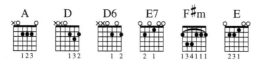

Verse 1

> **A**
> Standing on the promises of Christ my King,
>
> **D**   **A**
> Thro' eternal ages let His prais - es ring.
>
> Glory in the highest, I will shout and sing,
>
>   **D6**   **E7**   **A**
> Standing on the promis - es of God.

Chorus 1

> **A**   **D**   **F♯m**
> Standing, stand - ing,
>
> **E**   **A**   **D** **A**
> Standing on the promises of God my Sav - ior.
>
>   **D**
> Standing, standing,
>
>   **A**   **E7**   **A**
> I'm standing on the promis - es of God.

Verse 2

A
Standing on the promises that cannot fail,

D   A
When the howling storms of doubt and fear assail,

By the living Word of God I shall prevail,

          D6   E7   A
Standing on the promis - es of God.

Chorus 2   *Repeat Chorus 1*

Verse 3

A
Standing on the promises of Christ the Lord,

D   A
Bound to Him eternally by love's strong cord,

Overcoming daily with the Spirit's sword,

          D6   E7   A
Standing on the promis - es of God.

Chorus 3   *Repeat Chorus 1*

Verse 4

A
Standing on the promises I cannot fall,

D   A
List'ning every moment to the Spir - it's call,

Resting in my Savior as my all and all,

          D6   E7   A
Standing on the promis - es of God.

Chorus 4   *Repeat Chorus 1*

Sweet By and By

Words by Sanford Fillmore Bennett
Music by Joseph P. Webster

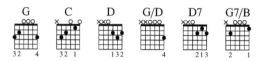

There's a land that is fair - er than day

G   C   D   G/D   D7   G7/B

Verse 1

            G   C   G
There's a land that is fairer than day

                          D
And by faith we can see it a - far.

            G   C   G
For the Father waits over the way

                C   G/D D   G
To prepare us a dwell - ing   place there.

Chorus 1

            G   D
In the sweet by and by,

            D7   G
We shall meet on that beautiful shore.

            G7/B C
In the sweet by and by,

            G   D7   G
We shall meet on that beautiful shore.

Verse 2

```
           G          C         G
We shall sing on that beautiful shore
                            D
The melodious songs of the blest,
           G          C         G
And our spirits shall sorrow no more,
               C     G/D D  G
Not a sigh for the bless - ing  of  rest.
```

Chorus 2   *Repeat Chorus 1*

Verse 3

```
           G        C        G
To our bountiful Father a - bove,
                           D
We will offer our tribute of praise
           G       C       G
For the glorious gift of His love
                   C   G/D D   G
And the blessings that hal - low  our days.
```

Chorus 3   *Repeat Chorus 1*

Sweet Hour of Prayer

Words by William W. Walford
Music by William B. Bradbury

Melody:

Sweet hour of prayer, sweet hour of prayer,

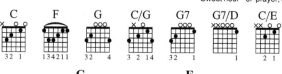

C   F   G   C/G   G7   G7/D   C/E

Verse 1

            C   F
Sweet hour of prayer, sweet hour of prayer,

        C   G   C/G G
That calls me from a world of   care,

        C   F
And bids me at my Father's throne

        C   G7 C
Make all my wants and wish - es known.

      G7/D C/E F   C
In sea - sons of   dis - tress and grief,

      G7/D C/E F C   G
My soul has   of - ten found re - lief

        C   F
And oft escaped the tempter's snare

        C   G7 C
By thy return, sweet hour of prayer.

Verse 2

            C   F
Sweet hour of prayer, sweet hour of prayer,

        C   G   C/G G
Thy joy I feel, the bliss I   share

        C   F
Of those whose anxious spirits burn

        C   G7 C
With strong desire for thy re - turn.

      G7/D C/E F C
With such I   has - ten to the place

      G7/D C/E F   C   G
Where God, my   Sav - ior, shows His face,

        C   F
And gladly take my station there

        C   G7 C
To wait for thee, sweet hour of prayer.

Verse 3

    C   F
Sweet hour of prayer, sweet hour of prayer,

    C   G C/G G
Thy wings shall my pe - ti - tion bear

    C   F
To Him whose truth and faithfulness

    C   G7 C
En - gage the waiting soul to   bless.

    G7/D C/E F   C
And sinse He   bids me seek His face,

    G7/D C/E   F   C   G
Believe His   Word and trust His grace,

    C   F
I'll cast on Him my ev'ry care

    C   G7 C
And wait for thee, sweet hour of   prayer.

Verse 4

    C   F
Sweet hour of prayer, sweet hour of prayer,

    C   G C/G G
May I thy conso - la - tion share,

    C   F
Till from Mount Pisgah's lofty height

   C   G7 C
I view my home and take my flight.

    G7/D C/E F C
This robe of   flesh I'll drop,

       G7/D C/E F   C   G
And rise to seize the   ev - er - lasting prize,

    C   F
And shout, while passing through the air,

    C   G7 C
"Fare - well, farewell, sweet hour of   prayer."

Tell It to Jesus

Words by Jeremiah E. Rankin
Music by Edmund S. Lorenz

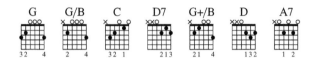

G	G/B	C	D7	G+/B	D	A7

Verse 1

G   G/B C   G
Are you wea - ry,   are you heavy hearted?

D7   G
Tell it to Jesus, tell it to Jesus.

G+/B C   G
Are you griev - ing   over joys de - parted?

D7   G
Tell it to Jesus a - lone.

Chorus 1

D   G   G/B
Tell it to Jesus, tell it to Je - sus,

C   G   D   A7   D   D7
He is a friend that's well - known.

G   G+/B C   G
You've no oth - er   such a friend or brother,

D7   G
Tell it to Jesus a - lone.

Verse 2

<pre>
G   G/B C   G
Do the tears flow down your cheeks un - bidden?

D7   G
Tell it to Jesus, tell it to Jesus.

            G+/B C   G
Have you sins that   to men's eyes are hidden?

D7   G
Tell it to Jesus a - lone.
</pre>

Chorus 2   *Repeat Chorus 1*

Verse 3

<pre>
G   G/B C   G
Do you fear the   gath'ring clouds of sorrow?

D7   G
Tell it to Jesus, tell it to Jesus.

            G+/B C   G
Are you anx - ious   what shall be to - morrow?

D7   G
Tell it to Jesus a - lone.
</pre>

Chorus 3   *Repeat Chorus 1*

Verse 4

<pre>
G   G/B C   G
Are you trou - bled at the thought of dying?

D7   G
Tell it to Jesus, tell it to Jesus.

            G+/B C   G
For Christ's com - ing   kingdom are you sighing?

D7   G
Tell it to Jesus a - lone.
</pre>

Chorus 4   *Repeat Chorus 1*

There Is a Fountain

Words by William Cowper
Traditional American Melody
Arranged by Lowell Mason

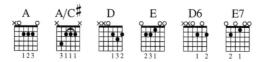

A   A/C#   D   E   D6   E7

Verse 1

       A   A/C# D   A
There is a foun - tain   filled with blood

                         E
Drawn from Immanuel's veins,

      A   A/C# D   A
And sinners plunged be - neath that flood

A/C# D6 A   E7   A
Lose _____ all their guilty stains,

           E   A D
Lose all their guilt - y stains,

      A   E
Lose all their guilty stains.

      A   A/C# D   A
And sinners plunged be - neath that flood

A/C# D6 A   E7   A
Lose _____ all their guilty stains.

Verse 2

```
        A      A/C♯ D      A
The dying thief re  -  joiced to see

                E
That fountain in his day,

        A         A/C♯ D    A
And there may I, though vile as he,

A/C♯ D6 A    E7     A
Wash ___ all my sins a - way,

          E   A  D
Wash all my sins a - way,

        A          E
Wash all my sins a - way.

        A         A/C♯ D    A
And there may I, though vile as he,

A/C♯ D6 A    E7     A
Wash ___ all my sins a - way.
```

Verse 3

```
        A          A/C♯ D     A
Dear dying Lamb, Thy   precious blood

                E
Shall never lose its pow'r,

        A          A/C♯ D       A
Till all the ran - somed Church of God

A/C♯ D6 A      E7    A
Be _____ saved to sin no more,

            E   A  D
Be saved to sin no more,

        A          E
Be saved to sin no more.

        A          A/C♯ D      A
Till all the ran - somed Church of God

A/C♯ D6 A      E7    A
Be _____ saved to sin no more.
```

Verse 4

```
        A           A/C# D      A
E'er since, by faith, I       saw the stream

                          E
Thy flowing wounds sup - ply,

        A           A/C# D      A
Re - deeming love has     been my theme

A/C# D6 A     E7   A
And ____ shall be till I die,

            E A D
And shall be till I   die,

      A           E
And shall be till I die.

      A           A/C# D      A
Re - deeming love has     been my theme

A/C# D6 A     E7   A
And ____ shall be till I die.
```

Verse 5

```
          A           A/C# D        A
When this poor lisp - ing,   stamm'ring  tongue

                E
Lies silent in the grave,

      A      A/C# D      A
Then in a no - bler,   sweeter song

A/C# D6 A      E7        A
I'll _____ sing Thy pow'r to save,

          E      A D
I'll sing Thy pow'r to  save,

      A              E
I'll sing Thy pow'r to save.

      A      A/C# D      A
Then in a no - bler,   sweeter song

A/C# D6 A      E7        A
I'll _____ sing Thy pow'r to save.
```

When I Can Read My Title Clear

Words by Isaac Watts
Traditional American Melody
Attributed to Joseph C. Lowry

Melody:

When I can read my title clear

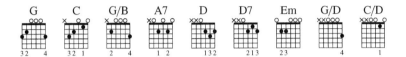

Verse 1

    G   **C G**
When I can read my title clear

    C G/B A7 D
To mansions in the skies,

   G   **D7**
I'll bid farewell to ev'ry fear

Em C   **G/D C/D D7 G**
And wipe my weep - ing _____ eyes.

          C G
And wipe my weeping eyes,

    C   **G/B A7 D**
And wipe my weep - ing eyes.

   G   **D7**
I'll bid farewell to ev'ry fear

Em C   **G/D C/D D7 G**
And wipe my weep - ing _____ eyes.

Verse 2

```
        G              C      G
Should earth against my soul en - gage,

        C   G/B A7   D
And fiery darts be    hurled,

    G                    D7
Then I can smile at Satan's rage

Em  C    G/D    C/D  D7  G
And  face a frown - ing ____ world.

                  C   G
And face a frowning world,

            C     G/B A7   D
And face a frown - ing    world.

    G                    D7
Then I can smile at Satan's rage

Em  C    G/D    C/D  D7  G
And  face a frown - ing ____ world.
```

Verse 3

```
        G              C    G
Let cares like a wild deluge come,

          C   G/B A7  D
And storms of sor - row  fall.

    G                  D7
May I but safely reach my home,

Em  C      G/D    C/D  D7  G
My   God, my heav'n, my ____ all.

                    C   G
My God, my heav'n, my all,

          C     G/B A7  D
My God, my heav'n, my   all.

    G                  D7
May I but safely reach my home,

Em  C      G/D    C/D  D7  G
My   God, my heav'n, my ____ all.
```

Verse 4

    G   **C** **G**
There shall I bathe my weary soul

       C   **G/B A7 D**
In seas of heav'n - ly   rest,

    G   **D7**
And not a wave of trouble roll

Em C   **G/D** **C/D D7 G**
A - cross my peace - ful _____ breast.

            C **G**
Across my peaceful breast,

      C   **G/B A7** **D**
Across my peace - ful   breast.

    G   **D7**
And not a wave of trouble roll

Em C   **G/D** **C/D D7 G**
A - cross my peace - ful _____ breast.

There Is Power in the Blood

Words and Music by
Lewis E. Jones

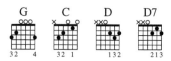

Verse 1

   G   C   G
Would you be free from your burden of sin?

       D   G
There's pow'r in the blood, pow'r in the blood.

                 C   G
Would you o'er evil a victory win?

      D7   G
There's wonderful pow'r in the blood.

Chorus 1

      G   C   G
There is pow'r, pow'r, wonderworking pow'r

   D7   G
In the blood of the Lamb.

               C   G
There is pow'r, pow'r, wonderworking pow'r

   D7   G   D7   G
In the precious blood of the Lamb.

| | G   C   G |

Verse 2

                          G   C   G

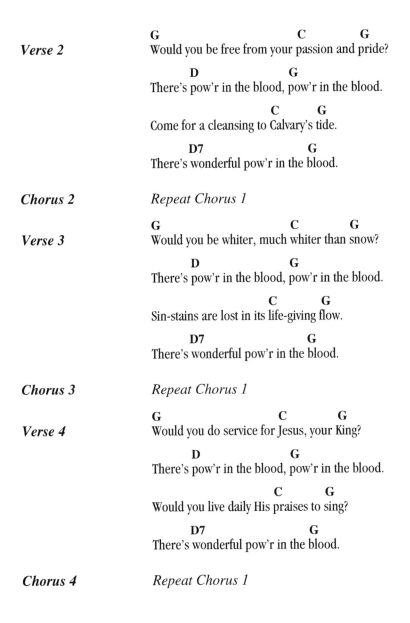

Verse 2

G   C   G
Would you be free from your passion and pride?

    D   G
There's pow'r in the blood, pow'r in the blood.

                     C   G
Come for a cleansing to Calvary's tide.

    D7   G
There's wonderful pow'r in the blood.

Chorus 2   *Repeat Chorus 1*

Verse 3

G   C   G
Would you be whiter, much whiter than snow?

    D   G
There's pow'r in the blood, pow'r in the blood.

                     C   G
Sin-stains are lost in its life-giving flow.

    D7   G
There's wonderful pow'r in the blood.

Chorus 3   *Repeat Chorus 1*

Verse 4

G   C   G
Would you do service for Jesus, your King?

    D   G
There's pow'r in the blood, pow'r in the blood.

                     C   G
Would you live daily His praises to sing?

    D7   G
There's wonderful pow'r in the blood.

Chorus 4   *Repeat Chorus 1*

'Tis So Sweet to Trust in Jesus

Words by Louisa M.R. Stead
Music by William J. Kirkpatrick

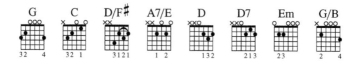

'Tis so sweet to trust in Je - sus,

G   C   D/F#   A7/E   D   D7   Em   G/B

Verse 1

G   C   G
'Tis so sweet to trust in Je - sus,

            D/F#   A7/E   D
Just to take Him at   His   Word.

G   C   G
Just to rest up - on His prom - ise,

          C   G   D   G
Just to know, "Thus saith the Lord."

Chorus 1

G   D7   Em   G   D
Jesus, Jesus, how I   trust Him.

G   D/F#   A7/E   D
How I've proved Him o'er   and   o'er.

G   G/B   C   G
Jesus, Je - sus,   precious Je - sus.

       C   G   D   G
O for grace to trust Him more.

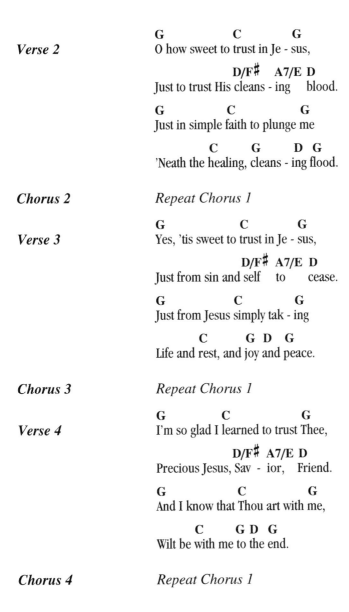

Verse 2

G   C   G
O how sweet to trust in Je - sus,

              D/F♯   A7/E D
Just to trust His cleans - ing   blood.

G   C   G
Just in simple faith to plunge me

          C   G   D G
'Neath the healing, cleans - ing flood.

Chorus 2

Repeat Chorus 1

Verse 3

G   C   G
Yes, 'tis sweet to trust in Je - sus,

              D/F♯ A7/E D
Just from sin and self   to   cease.

G   C   G
Just from Jesus simply tak - ing

          C   G D G
Life and rest, and joy and peace.

Chorus 3

Repeat Chorus 1

Verse 4

G   C   G
I'm so glad I learned to trust Thee,

              D/F♯ A7/E D
Precious Jesus, Sav - ior,   Friend.

G   C   G
And I know that Thou art with me,

          C   G D G
Wilt be with me to the end.

Chorus 4

Repeat Chorus 1

Turn Your Eyes Upon Jesus

Words and Music by
Helen H. Lemmel

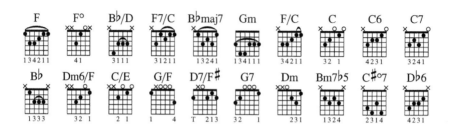

O soul, are you wea-ry and

Verse 1

  F F° F   B♭/D F7/C B♭maj7 Gm
O soul, are you wea - ry and troub - led?

  F/C C F/C C6 C7   F
No light in the dark - ness you see?

    F° F B♭ F Dm6/F C/E
There's light for a look at the Sav - ior,

C F G/F D7/F♯ C G7   C
And life more a - bun - dant and free.

Chorus 1

  F   C   C7 Dm F7/C
Turn your eyes up - on Je - sus.

   B♭   Bm7♭5 C
Look full in His wonder - ful face,

  F   C♯°7 Dm F7/C B♭
And the things of earth will grow strange - ly dim

Dm D♭6 F/C C F/C C7   F
In the light of His glory and grace.

Verse 2

         F   F° F   Bb/D F7/C Bbmaj7 Gm
Through death in - to life ev - er - last - ing

      F/C   C F/C C6 C7   F
He passed, and we   fol - low Him there.

          F° F Bb   F   Dm6/F C/E
Over us sin no more hath do - min - ion,

  C F   G/F D7/F♯ C   G7   C
For more ____ than   con - qu'rors we are.

Chorus 2   *Repeat Chorus 1*

Verse 3

         F   F°   F   Bb/D F7/C Bbmaj7 Gm
His word shall not fail you,   He   prom - ised.

      F/C C   F/C C6 C7   F
Be - lieve Him, and all   will be well.

         F° F Bb   F   Dm6/F C/E
Then go to a world that is dy - ing,

  C   F   G/F D7/F♯ C G7   C
His per - fect sal - va - tion to tell.

Chorus 3   *Repeat Chorus 1*

The Unclouded Day

Words and Music by
J.K. Alwood

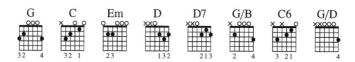

O they tell me of a home far be - yond the skies,

G   C   Em   D   D7   G/B   C6   G/D

Verse 1

               G   C   G
O they tell me of a home far be - yond the skies,

                             Em D
O they tell me of a home far a - way.

D7 G   **C**   **G**
O they tell me of a home were no storm clouds rise,

                G/B C6 G/D D7   **G**
O they tell me of   an un - clouded day.

Chorus 1

               G
O the land of cloudless day.

                          D
O the land of an unclouded day.

D7 G   **C**   **G**
O they tell me of a home were no storm clouds rise,

                G/B C6 G/D D7   **G**
O they tell me of   an un - clouded day.

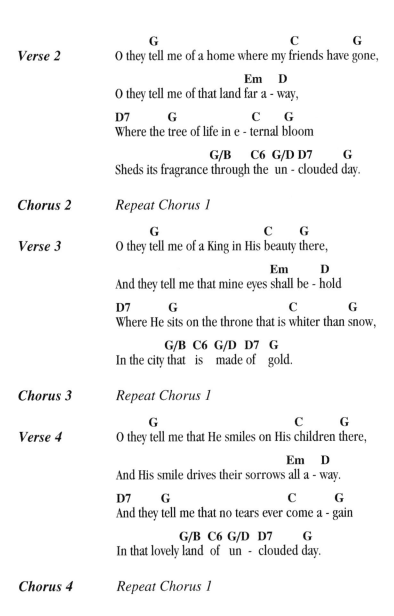

Verse 2
                    G   C   G
O they tell me of a home where my friends have gone,

                         Em   D
O they tell me of that land far a - way,

D7   G   C   G
Where the tree of life in e - ternal bloom

                    G/B   C6 G/D D7   G
Sheds its fragrance through the un - clouded day.

Chorus 2   *Repeat Chorus 1*

                    G   C   G
Verse 3   O they tell me of a King in His beauty there,

                              Em   D
And they tell me that mine eyes shall be - hold

D7   G   C   G
Where He sits on the throne that is whiter than snow,

           G/B C6 G/D D7 G
In the city that   is   made of   gold.

Chorus 3   *Repeat Chorus 1*

                    G   C   G
Verse 4   O they tell me that He smiles on His children there,

                              Em   D
And His smile drives their sorrows all a - way.

D7   G   C   G
And they tell me that no tears ever come a - gain

           G/B C6 G/D D7   G
In that lovely land of un - clouded day.

Chorus 4   *Repeat Chorus 1*

Wayfaring Stranger

Southern American Folk Hymn

Melody:

I am a poor _____ way-far-ing stran-ger...

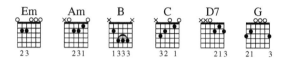

Em   Am   B   C   D7   G
23   231   1333 32 1 213   21 3

            Em

Verse 1   I am a poor wayfaring stranger

                    Am   **B**

While trav'ling through this world of woe,

Yet there's no sickness, toil, nor danger

                 Am   **Em**

In that bright world to which I go.

              C   **D7**   **G**

I'm going there to see my Father,

              C   **D7** **Em**

I'm going there no more to roam;

I'm only going over Jordan,

              Am   **Em**

I'm only going over home.

Verse 2

          Em
I know dark clouds will gather 'round me,

         Am   **B**
I know my way is rough and steep;

But golden fields lie out before me

          Am   **Em**
Where God's re-deemed shall ever sleep.

        C   **D7**   **G**
I'm going there to see my mother,

           C   **D7** **Em**
She said she'd meet me when I come;

I'm only going over Jordan,

        Am   **Em**
I'm only going over home.

Verse 3

          Em
I'll soon be free from ev'ry trial,

         Am   **B**
My body sleep in the church-yard;

I'll drop the cross of self-denial

         Am   **Em**
And enter on my greatest re-ward.

        C   **D7**   **G**
I'm going there to see my Savior,

         C   **D7** **Em**
To sing His praise for-ever-more;

I'm only going over Jordan,

        Am   **Em**
I'm only going over home.

We'll Understand It Better By and By

Words and Music by
Charles A. Tindley

Tri-als dark on ev-'ry hand, and we can-not un-der-stand

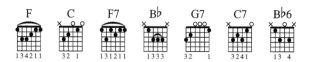

F C F7 Bb G7 C7 Bb6
134211 32 1 131211 1333 32 1 3241 13 4

Verse 1

　　　　　　　　　F　　　　　　　C　F7 Bb　　　　　F
Trials dark on ev'ry hand, and we cannot under - stand

　　　　　　　　　　　　　　　　　　　　　C　　G7　　　C7
All the ways that God would lead us to that blessed Promised Land.

　　　　　　　　F　　　　　　　　C　F7　Bb　　　　　F
But He'll guide us with His eye, and we'll follow till we die.

　　Bb6 F　　　　　C7　　　　　F
We will understand it better by and by.

Chorus 1

F　　　F7 Bb　　　　　　　F
By and by, ___ when the morning comes,

　　　　　　　　　　　C　　G7　　　C7
When the Saints of God are gathered home,

　　　　　　F　　　　F7 Bb　　　　　　F
We will tell the sto - ry how we've over - come,

G7　　F　　　　C7　　　　　F
We will understand it better by and by.

Verse 2
       F   C   F7 B♭   F

Oft our cherished plans have failed, dis - ap - pointments have pre - vailed,

                      C   G7   C7

And we've wandered in the darkness, heavy hearted and a - lone.

      F   C F7 B♭   F

But we're trusting in the Lord, and ac - cording to His Word,

  B♭6 F   C7   F

We will understand it better by and by.

Chorus 2   *Repeat Chorus 1*

Verse 3
       F   C F7 B♭   F

Temp - tations, hidden snares of - ten take us un - awares,

                        C   G7   C

And our hearts are made to bleed for some thoughtless word or deed.

      F   C   F7 B♭   F

And we wonder why the test when we try to do our best,

  B♭6 F   C7   F

But we'll understand it better by and by.

Chorus 3   *Repeat Chorus 1*

What a Friend We Have in Jesus

Words by Joseph M. Scriven
Music by Charles C. Converse

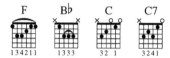

Verse 1

    F   B♭   F   B♭
What a Friend we have in Jesus,

    F   C
All our sins and grief to bear.

    F   B♭   F   B♭
What a priv - ilege to carry

    F   C7 F
Ev'rything to God in prayer.

    C   F
O what peace we often forfeit,

    B♭   F   C7 F C
O what needless pain we bear,

    F   B♭   F   B♭
All be - cause we do not carry

    F   C7 F
Ev'rything to God in prayer.

Verse 2

```
F       Bb  F            Bb
Have we tri - als and temp - tations?

F                    C
Is there trouble any - where?

F          Bb   F        Bb
We should nev - er be dis - couraged,

F                  C7  F
Take it to the Lord in   prayer.

C                      F
Can we find a friend so faithful

Bb      F     C7   F    C
Who will all our sor - rows share?

F    Bb     F        Bb
Jesus knows our ev'ry weakness,

F                  C7  F
Take it to the Lord in   prayer.
```

Verse 3

```
F    Bb    F         Bb
Are we weak and heavy laden,

F                      C
Cumbered with a load of care?

F       Bb   F          Bb
Precious Sav - ior, still our Refuge,

F                  C7  F
Take it to the Lord in   prayer.

C                          F
Do thy friends despise, for - sake thee?

Bb     F    C7    F  C
Take it to the Lord in prayer.

F    Bb   F             Bb
In His arms He'll take and shield thee,

F                  C7  F
Thou wilt find a sol - ace there.
```

When the Roll Is Called Up Yonder

Words and Music by
James M. Black

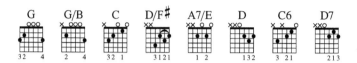

When the trum - pet of the Lord shall sound and

G   G/B   C   D/F♯   A7/E   D   C6   D7

Verse 1

              G   G/B   C   G
When the trumpet of the Lord shall sound and time shall be no more,

                               D/F♯ A7/E D
And the morning breaks, eternal, bright and   fair,

              G   G/B C   G
When the saved of earth shall gather over on the other shore,

G/B C6 G   D7   G
And   the roll is called up yonder, I'll be there.

Chorus 1

              G
When the roll is called up yonder,

              D7
When the roll is called up yonder,

              G   C
When the roll is called up yonder,

              G   D7   G
When the roll is called up yonder, I'll be there.

GUITAR CHORD SONGBOOK

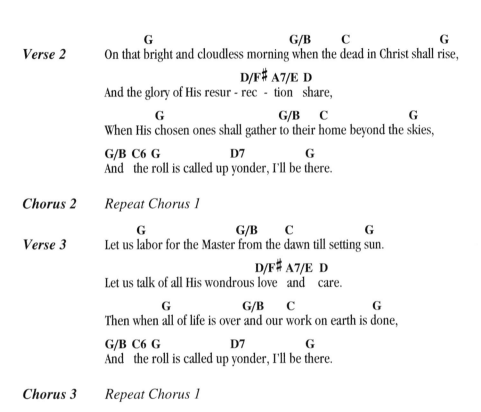

Verse 2
         G   G/B   C   G
On that bright and cloudless morning when the dead in Christ shall rise,

                      D/F♯ A7/E D
And the glory of His resur - rec - tion   share,

         G   G/B   C   G
When His chosen ones shall gather to their home beyond the skies,

G/B C6 G   D7   G
And   the roll is called up yonder, I'll be there.

Chorus 2   *Repeat Chorus 1*

                  G   G/B   C   G
Verse 3   Let us labor for the Master from the dawn till setting sun.

                      D/F♯ A7/E D
Let us talk of all His wondrous love   and   care.

         G   G/B   C   G
Then when all of life is over and our work on earth is done,

G/B C6 G   D7   G
And   the roll is called up yonder, I'll be there.

Chorus 3   *Repeat Chorus 1*

When the Saints Go Marching In

Words by Katherine E. Purvis
Music by James M. Black

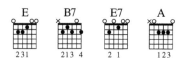

Verse 1

              E
Oh, when the saints go marching in,

                         B7
Oh, when the saints go marching in,

     E   **E7**   **A**
Oh Lord, I want to be in that number,

     E   **B7**   **E**
When the saints go marching in.

Verse 2

              E
Oh, when the sun refuse to shine,

                      B7
Oh, when the sun refuse to shine,

     E   **E7**   **A**
Oh Lord, I want to be in that number,

     E   **B7**   **E**
When the sun re-fuse to shine.

Verse 3   E
Oh, when they crown Him Lord of all,

                                       B7
Oh, when they crown Him Lord of all,

           E   E7   A
Oh Lord, I want to be in that number,

           E   B   E
When they crown Him Lord of all.

Verse 4   E
Oh, when they gather 'round the throne,

                                       B7
Oh, when they gather 'round the throne,

           E   E7   A
Oh Lord, I want to be in that number,

           E   B7   E
When they gather 'round the throne.

When We All Get to Heaven

Words by Eliza E. Hewitt
Music by Emily D. Wilson

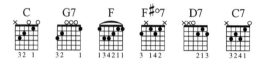

Sing   the   won‑d'rous   love __   of __   Je - sus,

C	G7	F	F#°7	D7	C7
32 1	32 1	1 3 4 2 1 1	3 1 4 2	2 1 3	3 2 4 1

Verse 1

C
Sing the wond'rous love of Jesus,

G7   C
Sing His mercy and His grace.

        F   F#°7
In the mansions bright and bless - ed

C G7   C
He'll pre - pare for us a place.

Chorus 1

       C
When we all get to heaven,

       D7   G7
What a day of re - joicing that will be.

    C C7 F
When we all see Jesus,

F#°7 C   G7   C F C
We'll sing and shout the victo - ry.

Verse 2

C
While we walk the pilgrim pathway

G7   C
Clouds will overspread the sky.

            F   F#°7
But when trav'ling days are o - ver,

C   G7   C
Not a shadow, not a sigh.

Chorus 2   *Repeat Chorus 1*

Verse 3
C
Let us then be true and faithful,

G7   C
Trusting, serving ev'ry day.

                    F   F#°7
Just one glimpse of Him in glo - ry

C   G7   C
Will the toils of life re - pay.

Chorus 3   *Repeat Chorus 1*

Verse 4
C
Onward to the prize before us.

G7   C
Soon His beauty we'll be - hold,

            F   F#°7
Soon the pearly gates will o - pen,

C   G7   C
We shall tread the streets of gold.

Chorus 4   *Repeat Chorus 1*

Whispering Hope

Words and Music by
Alice Hawthorne

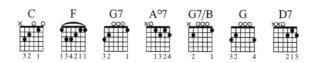

Verse 1

    C   F   C
Soft as the voice of an angel

G7   C
Breathing a lesson un - heard.

                  F
Hope with a gentle per - suasion

C   G7   C
Whispers her comforting word.

             A°7 G7/B C
Wait till the dark - ness is   over,

G   D7   G G7
Wait till the tempest is done.

C   F   C
Hope for the sunshine to - morrow

        G7   C
After the shower is gone.

Chorus 1

G7   C   G7   C
Whispering hope, O how welcome Thy voice,

F   C   G7   C
Making my heart in its sorrow re - joice.

<pre>
                              C   F   C
Verse 2   If, in the dusk of the twilight,

                              G7   C
                              Dim be the region a - far,

                                                  F
                              Will not the deepening darkness

                              C   G7   C
                              Brighten the glimmering star?

                                           A°7 G7/B C
                              Then when the night is   up - on us,

                              G   D7   G G7
                              Why should the heart sink a - way?

                              C   F   C
                              When the dark midnight is over,

                                        G7   C
                              Watch for the breaking of day.

Chorus 2   Repeat Chorus 1

                              C   F   C
Verse 3   Hope, as an anchor so steadfast,

                              G7   C
                              Rends the dark veil for the soul.

                                                  F
                              Whither the Master has entered,

                              C   G7   C
                              Robbing the grave of it's goal.

                                           A°7 G7/B C
                              Come then, O come, glad fru - ition,

                              G   D7   G G7
                              Come to my sad weary heart.

                              C   F   C
                              Come, O Thou blest hope of glory,

                                        G7   C
                              Never, O never de - part.

Chorus 3   Repeat Chorus 1
</pre>

Whiter Than Snow

Words by James L. Nicholson
Music by William G. Fischer

Melody:

Lord   Je - sus, I   long   to be

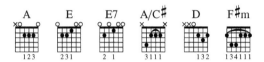

Verse 1

      A   E A   E7   A
Lord Jesus, I long to be perfectly whole,

          E   A   E7   A
I want Thee for - ever to live in my soul.

               A/C♯ D   A
Break down ev - 'ry   idol, cast out ev'ry foe.

                    E7   A
Now wash me and I shall be whiter than snow.

Chorus 1

E7   F♯m   D A
Whiter than snow, yes, whiter than snow.

   D   A   E7   A
Now wash me and I shall be whiter than snow.

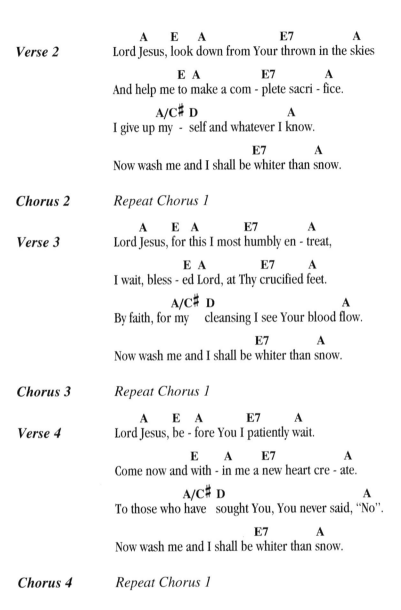

Verse 2

A   E   A   E7   A
Lord Jesus, look down from Your thrown in the skies

          E A   E7   A
And help me to make a com - plete sacri - fice.

       A/C♯ D   A
I give up my - self and whatever I know.

                   E7   A
Now wash me and I shall be whiter than snow.

Chorus 2   *Repeat Chorus 1*

Verse 3

A   E   A   E7   A
Lord Jesus, for this I most humbly en - treat,

         E A   E7   A
I wait, bless - ed Lord, at Thy crucified feet.

       A/C♯ D   A
By faith, for my   cleansing I see Your blood flow.

                 E7   A
Now wash me and I shall be whiter than snow.

Chorus 3   *Repeat Chorus 1*

Verse 4

A   E   A   E7   A
Lord Jesus, be - fore You I patiently wait.

         E   A   E7   A
Come now and with - in me a new heart cre - ate.

       A/C♯ D   A
To those who have   sought You, You never said, "No".

               E7   A
Now wash me and I shall be whiter than snow.

Chorus 4   *Repeat Chorus 1*

Will the Circle Be Unbroken

Words by Ada R. Habershon
Music by Charles H. Gabriel

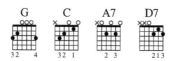

I was stand-ing by my win-dow

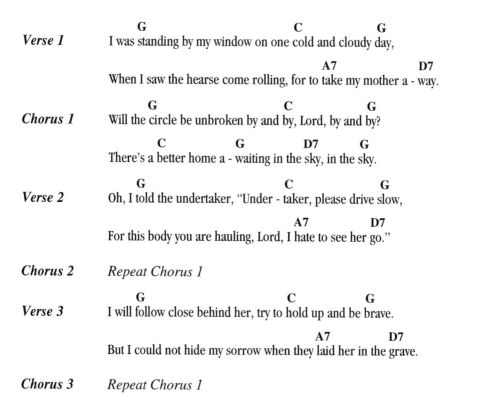

Verse 1

      G   C   G
I was standing by my window on one cold and cloudy day,

                              A7   D7
When I saw the hearse come rolling, for to take my mother a - way.

Chorus 1

     G   C   G
Will the circle be unbroken by and by, Lord, by and by?

       C   G   D7   G
There's a better home a - waiting in the sky, in the sky.

Verse 2

     G   C   G
Oh, I told the undertaker, "Under - taker, please drive slow,

                             A7   D7
For this body you are hauling, Lord, I hate to see her go."

Chorus 2   *Repeat Chorus 1*

Verse 3

     G   C   G
I will follow close behind her, try to hold up and be brave.

                             A7   D7
But I could not hide my sorrow when they laid her in the grave.

Chorus 3   *Repeat Chorus 1*

Wonderful Grace of Jesus

Words and Music by
Haldor Lillenas

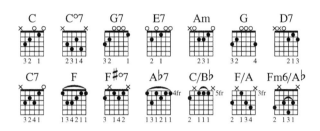

Verse 1

C   C°7 C
Wonderful grace of Je - sus,

     G7 C E7
Greater than all my sin.

Am
How shall my tongue describe it?

G   D7   G G7
Where shall its praise be - gin?

C   C°7 C
Taking away my bur - den,

     C7 F
Setting my spirit free.

Chorus 1

           F#°7   D7   C A♭7
For the wonderful grace of Je - sus

C   G7 C
Reach - es me.

                      G7
Wonderful, the matchless grace of Jesus,

C   G7
Deeper than the mighty rolling sea.

                 C
Higher than the mountain, sparkling like a fountain.

D7   G
All sufficient grace for even me.

C   G
Broader than the scope of my trans - gressions,

C   C7   F
Greater far than all my sin and shame.

  F#°7   C   C/B♭ F/A Fm6/A♭
O magnify the precious name of   Je - sus,

C   G7 C
Praise His name.

	C C°7 C

Verse 2

C   C°7 C
Wonderful grace of Je - sus,

              G7   C E7
Reaching to all the lost.

Am
By it I have been pardoned,

G   **D7**   **G** **G7**
Saved to the utter - most.

C   **C°7** **C**
Chains have been torn a - sun - der,

              C7   **F**
Giving me liber - ty.

Chorus 2   *Repeat Chorus 1*

Verse 3

C   **C°7** **C**
Wonderful grace of Je - sus,

              G7   **C** **E7**
Reaching the most de - filed.

Am
By its transforming power,

G   **D7**   **G** **G7**
Making him God's dear child.

C   **C°7** **C**
Purchasing peace and heav - en

             C7   **F**
For all e - terni - ty.

Chorus 3   *Repeat Chorus 1*

Wonderful Peace

Words by W.D. Cornell
Music by W.G. Cooper

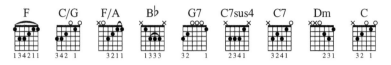

Verse 1

           F   C/G F/A B♭   F
Far a - way in the depths of my spirit to - night

            G7   C7sus4 C7
Rolls a melody sweeter than psalm.

          F   C/G F/A B♭
In ce - lestial like strains it   un - ceasingly falls

        F   C7   F
O'er my soul like an in - finite calm.

Chorus 1

 F   F/A B♭   F
Peace! Peace! Wonderful peace,

        Dm   G7   C
Coming down from the Father a - bove.

        F   C/G F/A B♭
Sweep over my spir - it   for - ever, I pray,

      F   C7   F
In fathomless billows of love.

Verse 2

            F   C/G F/A B♭   F
What a treasure I have in   this wonderful peace,

           G7   C7sus4 C7
Buried deep in the heart of my soul.

         F   C/G F/A B♭
So se - cure that no pow - er   can mine it away,

        F   C7   F
While the years of e - ternity roll.

Chorus 2   *Repeat Chorus 1*

Verse 3

        F   C/G F/A B♭   F
I am resting tonight in   this   wonderful peace,

               G7   C7sus4 C7
Resting sweetly in Jesus' con - trol.

        F   C/G F/A B♭
For I'm kept from all dan - ger by   night and by day,

        F   C7   F
And His glory is flooding my soul.

Chorus 3   *Repeat Chorus 1*

Verse 4

        F   C/G F/A B♭   F
And me thinks when I rise to   that city of peace,

               G7   C7sus4 C7
Where the Author of peace I shall see,

        F   C/G F/A B♭
That one strain of the song which the ransomed will sing,

        F   C7   F
In that heavenly kingdom will be,

Chorus 4   *Repeat Chorus 1*

Verse 5

        F   C/G F/A B♭   F
Ah, soul, are you here with - out   comfort or rest,

               G7   C7sus4 C7
Marching down the rough pathway of time?

        F   C/G F/A B♭
Make Jesus your friend ere   the   shadows grow dark.

        F   C7   F
O ac - cept of this peace so sub - lime.

Chorus 5   *Repeat Chorus 1*

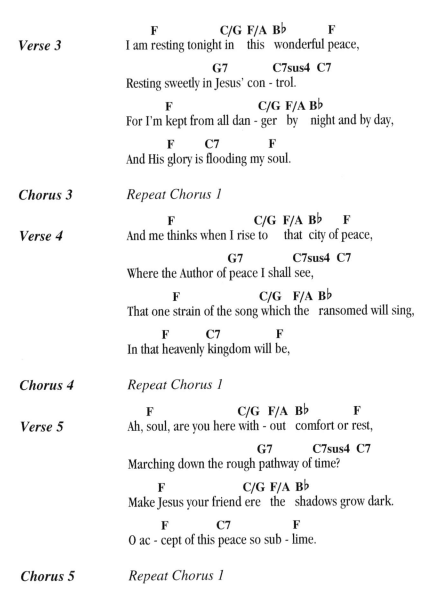

Wondrous Love

Southern American Folk Hymn

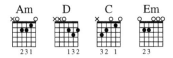

Verse 1

Am D   Am   C
What wondrous love is this,

Em   Am C   Em
Oh, my soul, oh, my soul.

C   Em   C
What wondrous love is this,

Em   Am
Oh, my soul!

D   Em   Am
What wondrous love is this

    Em   C   Am
That caused the Lord of Bliss

D Am   C
To bear the dreadful curse

Em   Am   Em
For my soul, for my soul,

    C   Em   Am
To bear the dreadful curse for my soul.

Verse 2

D   Am   C
What wondrous love is this,

Em   Am C   Em
Oh, my soul, oh, my soul.

C   Em   C
What wondrous love is this,

Em   Am
Oh, my soul!

D   Em   Am
What wondrous love is this

     Em   C   Am
That caused the Lord of Life

D Am   C
To lay aside His crown

Em   Am   Em
For my soul, for my soul,

  C   Em   Am
To lay aside His crown for my soul!

Verse 3

D Am   C
To God and to the Lamb

Em Am C   Em
I will sing, I will sing,

C Em   C
To God and to the Lamb

Em Am
I will sing.

D Em   Am
To God and to the Lamb

   Em C   Am
Who is the Great I AM.

D   Am   C
While millions join the theme

Em Am   Em
I will sing, I will sing,

   C   Em   Am
While millions join the theme I will sing.

Verse 4

D   Am   C
And when from death I'm free,

Em   Am C   Em
I'll sing on, I'll sing on.

C   Em   C
And when from death I'm free,

Em   Am
I'll sing on.

D   Em   Am
And when from death I'm free,

   Em   C   Am
I'll sing and joyful be,

D   Am   C
And through eterni - ty

Em   Am   Em
I'll sing on, I'll sing on,

      C   Em   Am
And through eterni - ty I'll sing on.

Guitar Chord Songbooks

Each book includes complete lyrics, chord symbols, and guitar chord diagrams.

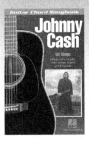 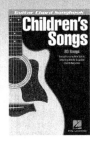  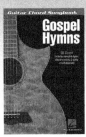 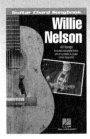

Acoustic Hits
More than 60 songs: Against the Wind • Name • One • Southern Cross • Take Me Home, Country Roads • Teardrops on My Guitar • Who'll Stop the Rain • Ziggy Stardust • and more.
00701787 ....$14.99

Acoustic Rock
80 acoustic favorites: Blackbird • Blowin' in the Wind • Layla • Maggie May • Me and Julio down by the Schoolyard • Pink Houses • and more.
00699540..................................$21.99

Alabama
50 of Alabama's best: Angels Among Us • The Closer You Get • If You're Gonna Play in Texas (You Gotta Have a Fiddle in the Band) • Mountain Music • When We Make Love • and more.
00699914..................................$14.95

The Beach Boys
59 favorites: California Girls • Don't Worry Baby • Fun, Fun, Fun • Good Vibrations • Help Me Rhonda • Wouldn't It Be Nice • dozens more!
00699566..................................$19.99

The Beatles
100 more Beatles hits: Lady Madonna • Let It Be • Ob-La-Di, Ob-La-Da • Paperback Writer • Revolution • Twist and Shout • When I'm Sixty-Four • and more.
00699562..................................$17.99

Bluegrass
Over 40 classics: Blue Moon of Kentucky • Foggy Mountain Top • High on a Mountain Top • Keep on the Sunny Side • Wabash Cannonball • The Wreck of the Old '97 • and more.
00702585..................................$14.99

Johnny Cash
58 Cash classics: A Boy Named Sue • Cry, Cry, Cry • Daddy Sang Bass • Folsom Prison Blues • I Walk the Line • Ring of Fire • Solitary Man • and more.
00699648..................................$17.99

Children's Songs
70 songs for kids: Alphabet Song • Bingo • The Candy Man • Eensy Weensy Spider • Puff the Magic Dragon • Twinkle, Twinkle Little Star • and more.
00699539..................................$16.99

Christmas Carols
80 Christmas carols: Angels We Have Heard on High • The Holly and the Ivy • I Saw Three Ships • Joy to the World • O Holy Night • and more.
00699536..................................$12.99

Christmas Songs
80 songs: All I Want for Christmas Is My Two Front Teeth • Baby, It's Cold Outside • Jingle Bell Rock • Mistletoe and Holly • Sleigh Ride • and more.
00119911..................................$14.99

Eric Clapton
75 of Slowhand's finest: I Shot the Sheriff • Knockin' on Heaven's Door • Layla • Strange Brew • Tears in Heaven • Wonderful Tonight • and more.
00699567 ....$19.99

Classic Rock
80 rock essentials: Beast of Burden • Cat Scratch Fever • Hot Blooded • Money • Rhiannon • Sweet Emotion • Walk on the Wild Side • and more.
00699598 ....$18.99

Coffeehouse Hits
57 singer-songwriter hits: Don't Know Why • Hallelujah • Meet Virginia • Steal My Kisses • Torn • Wonderwall • You Learn • and more.
00703318 ....$14.99

Country
80 country standards: Boot Scootin' Boogie • Crazy • Hey, Good Lookin' • Sixteen Tons • Through the Years • Your Cheatin' Heart • and more.
00699534 ....$17.99

Country Favorites
Over 60 songs: Achy Breaky Heart (Don't Tell My Heart) • Brand New Man • Gone Country • The Long Black Veil • Make the World Go Away • and more.
00700609 ....$14.99

Country Hits
40 classics: As Good As I Once Was • Before He Cheats • Cruise • Follow Your Arrow • God Gave Me You • The House That Built Me • Just a Kiss • Making Memories of Us • Need You Now • Your Man • and more.
00140859 ....$14.99

Country Standards
60 songs: By the Time I Get to Phoenix • El Paso • The Gambler • I Fall to Pieces • Jolene • King of the Road • Put Your Hand in the Hand • A Rainy Night in Georgia • and more.
00700608 ....$12.95

Cowboy Songs
Over 60 tunes: Back in the Saddle Again • Happy Trails • Home on the Range • Streets of Laredo • The Yellow Rose of Texas • and more.
00699636..................................$19.99

Creedence Clearwater Revival
34 CCR classics: Bad Moon Rising • Born on the Bayou • Down on the Corner • Fortunate Son • Up Around the Bend • and more.
00701786 ....$16.99

Jim Croce
37 tunes: Bad, Bad Leroy Brown • I Got a Name • I'll Have to Say I Love You in a Song • Operator (That's Not the Way It Feels) • Photographs and Memories • Time in a Bottle • You Don't Mess Around with Jim • and many more.
00148087 ....$14.99

Crosby, Stills & Nash
37 hits: Chicago • Dark Star • Deja Vu • Marrakesh Express • Our House • Southern Cross • Suite: Judy Blue Eyes • Teach Your Children • and more.
00701609.................................$16.99

John Denver
50 favorites: Annie's Song • Leaving on a Jet Plane • Rocky Mountain High • Take Me Home, Country Roads • Thank God I'm a Country Boy • and more.
02501697 ....$17.99

Neil Diamond
50 songs: America • Cherry, Cherry • Cracklin' Rosie • Forever in Blue Jeans • I Am...I Said • Love on the Rocks • Song Sung Blue • Sweet Caroline • and dozens more!
00700606 ....$19.99

Disney
56 super Disney songs: Be Our Guest • Friend like Me • Hakuna Matata • It's a Small World • Under the Sea • A Whole New World • Zip-A-Dee-Doo-Dah • and more.
00701071 ....$17.99

The Doors
60 classics from the Doors: Break on Through to the Other Side • Hello, I Love You (Won't You Tell Me Your Name?) • Light My Fire • Love Her Madly • Riders on the Storm • Touch Me • and more.
00699888 ....$17.99

Eagles
40 familiar songs: Already Gone • Best of My Love • Desperado • Hotel California • Life in the Fast Lane • Peaceful Easy Feeling • Witchy Woman • more.
00122917 ....$16.99

Early Rock
80 classics: All I Have to Do Is Dream • Big Girls Don't Cry • Fever • Itsy Bitsy Teenie Weenie Yellow Polkadot Bikini • Let's Twist Again • Lollipop • and more.
00699916 ....$14.99

Folk Pop Rock
80 songs: American Pie • Dust in the Wind • Me and Bobby McGee • Somebody to Love • Time in a Bottle • and more.
00699651 ....$17.99

Folksongs
80 folk favorites: Aura Lee • Camptown Races • Danny Boy • Man of Constant Sorrow • Nobody Knows the Trouble I've Seen • and more.
00699541 ....$14.99

40 Easy Strumming Songs
Features 40 songs: Cat's in the Cradle • Daughter • Hey, Soul Sister • Homeward Bound • Take It Easy • Wild Horses • and more.
00115972 ....$16.99

Four Chord Songs
40 hit songs: Blowin' in the Wind • I Saw Her Standing There • Should I Stay or Should I Go • Stand by Me • Turn the Page • Wonderful Tonight • and more.
00701611 ....$14.99

Glee
50+ hits: Bad Romance • Beautiful • Dancing with Myself • Don't Stop Believin' • Imagine • Rehab • Teenage Dream • True Colors • and dozens more.
00702501 ....$14.99

Gospel Hymns
80 hymns: Amazing Grace • Give Me That Old Time Religion • I Love to Tell the Story • Shall We Gather at the River? • Wondrous Love • and more.
00700463 ....$14.99

Grand Ole Opry®
80 great songs: Abilene • Act Naturally • Country Boy • Crazy • Friends in Low Places • He Stopped Loving Her Today • Wings of a Dove • dozens more!
00699885 ....$16.95

Grateful Dead
30 favorites: Casey Jones • Friend of the Devil • High Time • Ramble on Rose • Ripple • Rosemary • Sugar Magnolia • Truckin' • Uncle John's Band • more.
00139461 ....$14.99

Green Day
34 faves: American Idiot • Basket Case • Boulevard of Broken Dreams • Good Riddance (Time of Your Life) • 21 Guns • Wake Me Up When September Ends • When I Come Around • and more.
00103074 ....$14.99

Irish Songs
45 Irish favorites: Danny Boy • Girl I Left Behind Me • Harrigan • I'll Tell Me Ma • The Irish Rover • My Wild Irish Rose • When Irish Eyes Are Smiling • and more!
00701044 ....$14.99

Michael Jackson
27 songs: Bad • Beat It • Billie Jean • Black or White (Rap Version) • Don't Stop 'Til You Get Enough • The Girl Is Mine • Man in the Mirror • Rock with You • Smooth Criminal • Thriller • more.
00137847 ....$14.99

Billy Joel
60 Billy Joel favorites: • It's Still Rock and Roll to Me • The Longest Time • Piano Man • She's Always a Woman • Uptown Girl • We Didn't Start the Fire • You May Be Right • and more.
00699632 ....$19.99

Elton John
60 classics: Bennie and the Jets • Candle in the Wind • Crocodile Rock • Goodbye Yellow Brick Road • Sad Songs Say So Much • Tiny Dancer • Your Song • more.
00699732 ....$15.99

Ray LaMontagne
20 songs: Empty • Gossip in the Grain • Hold You in My Arms • I Still Care for You • Jolene • Trouble • You Are the Best Thing • and more.
00130337.................................$12.99

Latin Songs
60 favorites: Bésame Mucho (Kiss Me Much) • The Girl from Ipanema (Garôta De Ipanema) • The Look of Love • So Nice (Summer Samba) • and more.
00700973 ....$14.99

Love Songs
65 romantic ditties: Baby, I'm-A Want You • Fields of Gold • Here, There and Everywhere • Let's Stay Together • Never My Love • The Way We Were • more!
00701043.................................$14.99

Bob Marley
36 songs: Buffalo Soldier • Get up Stand Up • I Shot the Sheriff • Is This Love • No Woman No Cry • One Love • Redemption Song • and more.
00701704.................................$17.99

Bruno Mars
15 hits: Count on Me • Grenade • If I Knew • Just the Way You Are • The Lazy Song • Locked Out of Heaven • Marry You • Treasure • When I Was Your Man • and more.
00125332 ....$12.99

Paul McCartney
60 from Sir Paul: Band on the Run • Jet • Let 'Em In • Maybe I'm Amazed • No More Lonely Nights • Say Say Say • Take It Away • With a Little Luck • and more!
00385035 ....$16.95

Steve Miller
33 hits: Dance Dance Dance • Jet Airliner • The Joker • Jungle Love • Rock'n Me • Serenade from the Stars • Swingtown • Take the Money and Run • and more.
00701146.................................$12.99

Modern Worship
80 modern worship favorites: All Because of Jesus • Amazed • Everlasting God • Happy Day • I Am Free • Jesus Messiah • and more.
00701801 ....$16.99

Motown
60 Motown masterpieces: ABC • Baby I Need Your Lovin' • I'll Be There • Stop! In the Name of Love • You Can't Hurry Love • and more.
00699734 ....$17.99

Willie Nelson
44 favorites: Always on My Mind • Beer for My Horses • Blue Skies • Georgia on My Mind • Help Me Make It Through the Night • On the Road Again • Whiskey River • and many more.
00148273 ....$17.99

Nirvana
40 songs: About a Girl • Come as You Are • Heart Shaped Box • The Man Who Sold the World • Smells like Teen Spirit • You Know You're Right • and more.
00699762 ....$16.99

Roy Orbison
38 songs: Blue Bayou • Oh, Pretty Woman • Only the Lonely (Know the Way I Feel) • Working for the Man • You Got It • and more.
00699752 ....$17.99

Peter, Paul & Mary
43 favorites: If I Had a Hammer (The Hammer Song) • Leaving on a Jet Plane • Puff the Magic Dragon • This Land Is Your Land • and more.
00103013..................................$19.99

Tom Petty
American Girl • Breakdown • Don't Do Me like That • Free Fallin' • Here Comes My Girl • Into the Great Wide Open • Mary Jane's Last Dance • Refugee • Runnin' Down a Dream • The Waiting • and more.
00699883 ....$15.99

Pink Floyd
30 songs: Another Brick in the Wall, Part 2 • Brain Damage • Breathe • Comfortably Numb • Hey You • Money • Mother • Run like Hell • Us and Them • Wish You Were Here • Young Lust • and many more.
00139116 ....$14.99

Pop/Rock
80 chart hits: Against All Odds • Come Sail Away • Every Breath You Take • Hurts So Good • Kokomo • More Than Words • Smooth • Summer of '69 • and more.
00699538 ....$16.99

Praise and Worship
80 favorites: Agnus Dei • He Is Exalted • I Could Sing of Your Love Forever • Lord, I Lift Your Name on High • More Precious Than Silver • Open the Eyes of My Heart • Shine, Jesus, Shine • and more.
00699634 ....$14.99

Elvis Presley
60 hits: All Shook Up • Blue Suede Shoes • Can't Help Falling in Love • Heartbreak Hotel • Hound Dog • Jailhouse Rock • Suspicious Minds • Viva Las Vegas • and more.
00699633 ....$17.99

Queen
40 hits: Bohemian Rhapsody • Crazy Little Thing Called Love • Fat Bottomed Girls • Killer Queen • Tie Your Mother Down • Under Pressure • You're My Best Friend • and more!
00702395 ....$14.99

Red Hot Chili Peppers
50 hits: Californication • Give It Away • Higher Ground • Love Rollercoaster • Scar Tissue • Suck My Kiss • Under the Bridge • and more.
00699710 ....$19.99

The Rolling Stones
35 hits: Angie • Beast of Burden • Fool to Cry • Happy • It's Only Rock 'N' Roll (But I Like It) • Miss You • Not Fade Away • Respectable • Rocks Off • Start Me Up • Time Is on My Side • Tumbling Dice • Waiting on a Friend • and more.
00137716 ....$17.99

Bob Seger
41 favorites: Against the Wind • Hollywood Nights • Katmandu • Like a Rock • Night Moves • Old Time Rock & Roll • You'll Accomp'ny Me • and more!
00701147..................................$12.99

Carly Simon
Nearly 40 classic hits, including: Anticipation • Haven't Got Time for the Pain • Jesse • Let the River Run • Nobody Does It Better • You're So Vain • and more.
00121011..................................$14.99

Sting
50 favorites from Sting and the Police: Don't Stand So Close to Me • Every Breath You Take • Fields of Gold • King of Pain • Message in a Bottle • Roxanne • and more.
00699921 ....$17.99

Taylor Swift
40 tunes: Back to December • Bad Blood • Blank Space • Fearless • Fifteen • I Knew You Were Trouble • Look What You Made Me Do • Love Story • Mean • Shake It Off • Speak Now • Wildest Dreams • and many more.
00263755..................................$16.99

Three Chord Acoustic Songs
30 acoustic songs: All Apologies • Blowin' in the Wind • Hold My Hand • Just the Way You Are • Ring of Fire • Shelter from the Storm • This Land Is Your Land • and more.
00123860 ....$14.99

Three Chord Songs
65 includes: All Right Now • La Bamba • Lay Down Sally • Mony, Mony • Rock Around the Clock • Rock This Town • Werewolves of London • You Are My Sunshine • and more.
00699720 ....$17.99

Two-Chord Songs
Nearly 60 songs: ABC • Brick House • Eleanor Rigby • Fever • Paperback Writer • Ramblin' Man Tulsa Time • When Love Comes to Town • and more.
00119236..................................$16.99

U2
40 U2 songs: Beautiful Day • Mysterious Ways • New Year's Day • One • Sunday Bloody Sunday • Walk On • Where the Streets Have No Name • With or Without You • and more.
00137744..................................$14.99

Hank Williams
68 classics: Cold, Cold Heart • Hey, Good Lookin' • Honky Tonk Blues • I'm a Long Gone Daddy • Jambalaya (On the Bayou) • Your Cheatin' Heart • and more.
00700607 ....$16.99

Stevie Wonder
40 of Stevie's best: For Once in My Life • Higher Ground • Isn't She Lovely • My Cherie Amour • Sir Duke • Superstition • Uptight (Everything's Alright) • Yester-Me, Yester-You, Yesterday • and more!
00120862 ....$14.99

HAL•LEONARD®

Prices, contents and availability subject to change without notice.

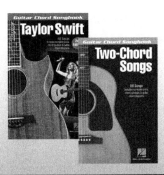